MEASURING GLOBALIZATION
FRAMEWORK, ANALYSIS, AND IMPLICATIONS

DECEMBER 2023

ASIAN DEVELOPMENT BANK

ADB

Contents

Tables, Figures, and Boxes

TABLES

FIGURES

Foreword

Globalization has helped deliver remarkable development outcomes for Asia and the Pacific. It has also featured prominently in recent debates on two key questions: how globalization might exacerbate inequalities and how it might accelerate climate change. To fully understand these possible impacts, a comprehensive measure that captures the scale, mode, and pace of globalization and that enables us to examine its complexities is essential.

This report introduces the Global Integration Index, which assesses the progress of globalization across traditional areas, such as trade, investment, and institutional arrangements, as well as in new areas such as digital connectivity and environmental cooperation. Building on the framework of the Asian Development Bank (ADB) to measure progress in regional cooperation and integration, the index confirms Asia's deeper global economic linkages and enables comparison with other regions and across different dimensions of globalization.

The new index recognizes the transformative role of digitalization and the need for global cooperation to address the challenge of climate change. Digital technologies can catalyze momentum for economic development in the region while environmental cooperation recognizes the necessity of global coordination to successfully protect an essential global public good.

The report also explores the potential role of regional integration in supporting globalization. There is much discussion today about deglobalization, derisking, and fragmentation, which could impact development prospects for the region, and especially smaller economies. And yet, in contrast to global narratives, regional integration within Asia and the Pacific continues to deepen, reflecting the continued commitment by pragmatic leaders in the region to open trade and investment. Regional agreements like the Regional Comprehensive Economic Partnership and the Comprehensive and Progressive Agreement for Trans-Pacific Partnership, and initiatives such as the Indo-Pacific Economic Framework, provide platforms to deepen economic collaboration. This remains core to ADB's mission and a fundamental driver underlying investments and technical assistance.

The Global Integration Index can be a valuable tool to explore how global and regional integration contribute to development outcomes. ADB recognizes the importance of assessing the benefits and costs of globalization and the need to design policies that account for these effects. This work reflects our commitment to providing tools for rethinking globalization and maximizing its potential for development.

Albert Park
Chief Economist and Director General
Economic Research and Development Impact Department
Asian Development Bank

Acknowledgments

The publication was prepared by the Regional Cooperation and Integration Division (ERCI) of the Economic Research and Development Impact Department (ERDI) of the Asian Development Bank (ADB), with support from Technical Assistance (TA) 9763: Enhancing the Measures of Regional Cooperation and Integration: The Asia-Pacific Regional Cooperation and Integration Index (ARCII).

The preparation of this report was led by Rolando Avendano (economist, ERCI), with the support of TA-9763 consultants or resource persons: Lovely Ann Tolin, Ryan Jacildo, Angelica Beatrice Natividad, and Kristine Anne Gloria.

The global integration index framework and estimates were based on the research led by Hyeon-Seung Huh (professor, Yonsei University), with advice from Cyn-Young Park (director, Regional Cooperation and Integration and Trade Division, Climate Change and Sustainable Development Department, ADB) and inputs from Rolando Avendano, Lovely Ann Tolin, and Ryan Jacildo. ADB consultants from TA-6753 Asian Economic Integration: Building Knowledge for Policy Dialogue, 2021–2023 (Subproject 2) provided data support: Carlos Cabaero, Clemence Cruz, Pilar Dayag, Joshua Gapay, Ana Kristel Lapid, Ma. Concepcion Latoja, and Pia Medrano.

The report team is grateful for the helpful feedback provided by Jong Woo Kang (director, ERCI) and participants at the (i) 17th International Convention of the East Asian Economic Association session on "Regional Integration in Asia and the Pacific: Spillovers and Future Trends" held on 28 August 2022 in Kuala Lumpur, and (ii) Asian Economic Development Conference held on 15 July 2023 at University of Tokyo.

Rolando Avendano and Mara Claire Tayag (senior economics officer, ERCI) coordinated the production of this report, with administrative support from Carol Ongchangco (operations coordinator, ERCI). Carol Ongchangco and Marilyn Parra (senior operations assistant, ERCI) provided logistics support in organizing the workshops and seminars.

James Unwin edited the report. Joseph Manglicmot typeset and produced the layout, and Erickson Mercado created the cover design. Tuesday Soriano proofread the report. Carol Ongchangco helped in proofreading the report. Support for printing and publishing was provided by the Printing Services Unit of ADB's Corporate Services Department and by the publishing team of the Department of Communications and Knowledge Management.

Abbreviations

ADB	Asian Development Bank
ADO	Asian Development Outlook
AFTA	ASEAN Free Trade Area
ARCII	Asia-Pacific Regional Cooperation and Integration Index
ASEAN	Association of Southeast Asian Nations
BIMP-EAGA	Brunei Darussalam-Indonesia-Malaysia-Philippines East ASEAN Growth Area
CAREC	Central Asia Regional Economic Cooperation
CO_2	carbon dioxide
EEII	Extraregional Economic Integration Index
EII	Extraregional Integration Index
ERDI	Economic Research and Development Impact
EU	European Union
FDI	foreign direct investment
FTA	free trade agreement
GEII	Global Economic Integration Index
GII	Global Integration Index
GMS	Greater Mekong Subregion
ILO	International Labour Organization
IMF	International Monetary Fund
IMT-GT	Indonesia-Malaysia-Thailand Growth Triangle
OECD	Organisation for Economic Co-operation and Development
PCA	principal components analysis
PRC	People's Republic of China
RCI	regional cooperation and integration
RII	Regional Integration Index
SAARC	South Asian Association for Regional Cooperation
SASEC	South Asia Subregional Economic Cooperation
TA	Technical Assistance
UNCTAD	United Nations Conference on Trade and Development
US	United States
WDI	World Development Indicators
WIPO	World Intellectual Property Organization
WITS	World Integrated Trade Solution
WTO	World Trade Organization

Executive Summary

Globalization refers to the growing interdependence of economies brought about by cross-border flows in goods and services, investment, technology, people, and information. This shift has been characterized as offering a key strategy for economic growth and development. It has also stirred debate over the potential for globalization to deepen inequalities and damage social and institutional stability.

Recent trends are reshaping the globalization story. COVID-19, geopolitical tensions, and conflict have exposed the fragility of global linkages and underlined the risks of economic fragmentation. And still, digitalization, inclusiveness, and environmental sustainability are becoming critical pillars of globalization. They have created new areas for economic interdependencies and linkages. In tandem, regional cooperation and integration (RCI) has gathered pace as a mechanism to further expand linkages and coordinate policies among economies seeking to attain common objectives.

While studies have explored the roles of global or regional integration separately, few have assessed their complex relationship. This report presents a framework for measuring global and regional integration while capturing their commonalities and multifaceted dimensions. The Global Integration Index (GII) builds upon ADB's framework to measure regional integration (Huh and Park 2021) and is expanded to improve the measurement and scope of globalization. The new indicator system comprises 43 indicators in eight dimensions, including two new ones—technology and digital connectivity, and environmental cooperation. To ensure comparability, the Regional Integration Index (RII), which shares the same structure as the global index, is also constructed.

Global integration is deepest among high-income economies, and the gap with other income groups is substantial. By region, the European Union (EU) is the most globally integrated. Even as the index reveals a wide gap, other regions are catching up with the EU, and estimates for their global integration shows significant improvement occurred between 2006 and 2021. By dimension, the EU and North America are also the most globally integrated, recording the highest estimates in almost all dimensions. Consistent with previous studies, the GII suggests a strong link between economic interdependence and economic development. The results are consistent across all dimensions except for environmental cooperation.

Similar to the GII, regional integration increased across all income groups from 2006 to 2021, with higher income economies experiencing the fastest growth. RII scores in Asia and the Pacific are considerably more dispersed than in other regions, which underscores significant differences in economic integration within the region. In 2021, the EU had the deepest regional integration in almost all dimensions, and a wider gap with other regions for money and finance and institutional arrangements. Within subregions, Southeast Asia and East Asia were the most regionally integrated.

Regional, extraregional, and global integration strengthened from 2006 to 2021. Integration across these dimensions has improved across most economies globally. In general, high income economies are better integrated with their neighbors, while low income economies tend to forge more linkages with other regions. While the EU and North America are more integrated with their own region, Asia's integration has been driven by both regional and extraregional linkages. In other emerging regions, extraregional linkages are dominant. These trends highlight the important but different role of regionalization in the process of globalization for industrialized and developing economies.

Globalization and regionalization are intertwined and mutually dependent processes. The effects of globalization on development are complex and multifaceted, with multiple channels needing to be considered. While findings suggest that both global and regional integration support economic growth, the relationship with income inequality or inclusive growth is more nuanced. Understanding how the effects of globalization and regionalization are distributed across different income groups remains an essential question in this agenda for researchers and policymakers.

CHAPTER 1

The Evolving Concept of Globalization

1.1 Introduction

The term globalization generally describes how the movement of goods and services, capital, technology, and people integrates economies and makes them more interdependent. That process is often accompanied by institutional and social integration, through features such as the convergence of legal and regulatory standards as well as closer cultural proximity.

Globalization has helped deliver extraordinary development outcomes, including for Asia and the Pacific. Deeper global integration has contributed to the expansion of markets, enhanced resource allocation efficiency, improved productivity, and increased opportunities for investment. However, deeper economic interdependence is not without risk. Previous episodes of crisis contagion have shown how interconnectedness may speed up the transmission of cross-border shocks (ADB 2018). Globalized trade and supply chains have also opened up vulnerabilities, as seen during global health, food, and energy crises. Although major supply chain disruptions during the coronavirus disease (COVID-19) pandemic were a vivid reminder of vulnerabilities, concerns already had been raised on the potential of unbridled globalization to widen inequalities and worsen climate change outcomes. In recent years, perspectives on globalization have transformed.

Globalization trends have ebbed and flowed with changing policies and political support. International flows have generally extended over greater distances although the recent pace has slowed, implying a possible growth in regionalization (Altman and Bastian 2023). The notion of increasing decoupling and growing deglobalization has also gained traction. For instance, the participation of firms in global production chains has shifted and plans to outsource production dwindled, with friend-shoring surfacing as a viable strategy for some economies. During the COVID-19 pandemic, for example, calls for greater domestic production of personal protection equipment and export bans on vaccines and critical medical goods and food were common. And, as seen in recent periods of economic uncertainty, global unease has given rise to protectionism (Arslan et al. 2018; IMF 2022a, 2022b).

On the other hand, the number of regional trade agreements continues to increase and new forms of integration such as digitalization and services trade are emerging. Rather than a wholesale move away from global integration, the process is likely to take different routes. Increased regionalization through regional trade agreements and deepening of regional supply chains are now contributing to a reshaping of the process. Calls have also intensified for stronger global governance to guide globalization through policies focused on social inclusion and environmental sustainability.

The absence of effective global governance systems and persistent inequalities has cast doubt on the future of globalization. One contention against unfettered globalization is that it may hasten cross-border crisis contagion, as seen during recent financial crises; that it opens doors for illicit capital flows and so calls into question the aptness and dexterity of macroprudential frameworks. Globalization, having opened local markets to competition from foreign products and firms as well as labor migration, is also provoking strong reaction in some economies. Local players are struggling to compete and migration has tightened domestic labor markets. Responding to this, changing policies are exemplified by rising trade barriers, reshoring and nearshoring measures, and stronger rules on migration.

Together with potential economic impacts, there is also a rising concern on the challenges that globalization poses for individuals and society. Besides environmental concerns, economic and social inequalities have come to the fore. The distributional impact of globalization is made tangible by the widening of income inequalities between and within economies and a deepening of political polarization (Bourguignon 2016; Milavonic 2016; Huh and Park 2021). Increasing trade is also seen as exacerbating industry pollution and carbon emissions which, in turn, undermine economic sustainability (WTO 2022). Concerted efforts to decarbonize trade and investment through national frameworks and multilateral agreements are therefore crucial in mitigating and adapting to climate change risks.

Technological progress is somehow countering the creeping deglobalization in traditional channels. Digitalization arguably blurs national borders. The cost of moving capital from one jurisdiction to another has fallen and the same goes for trade and labor through e-commerce and online work. Whereas technology has created new avenues for globalization, it has created additional regulatory concerns such as data privacy and ownership, cybersecurity, and the digital preparedness of users. Although technology can make globalization more inclusive, sustainable, and resilient, this is not preordained and requires concerted effort by policymakers.

Globalization is a constantly evolving process. While global integration may bring risks, economies can turn challenges into opportunities by taking advantage of its multifaceted nature. Global cooperation will be key to tackling transnational challenges such as global health and financial crises, energy and food security, climate change, and achieving goals for sustainable development. Increased economic and financial interdependencies also mean that overcoming these transnational challenges requires greater coordination of economic, social, and environmental policies globally, along with political commitment. It also demands more financial and technical resources than any single economy can provide alone.

1.2   Recent Trends: Geopolitical Tensions, COVID-19, and the Rise of Protectionism

The COVID-19 pandemic, the Russian invasion of Ukraine, and recent evidence of economic polarization between the United States (US) and the People's Republic of China (PRC) are among developments that continue to shape globalization. These events have exposed the lines of global fragmentation and disrupted established economic linkages, from global supply chains to the free movement of people. Questions on whether international flows are starting to reverse, suggesting a period of deglobalization, are emerging. Geopolitical tensions have also started to influence debate over whether increased regionalization trends may lead the global economy to split into rival blocs.

Although global tensions have grown and recent economic shocks have hit some economies hard, evidence suggests that international flows are not in retreat (Altman and Bastian 2023). International trade in goods and services and foreign direct investment (FDI) were affected during the COVID-19 pandemic and altered by geopolitical issues, but both have recovered gradually to pre-pandemic levels. International flows are expected to continue to grow, though at a slower pace than in previous years as economic conditions remain difficult amid persistent inflation and monetary tightening. As of today, evidence on trade, investment, and global value chains does not support the notion that the world economy has fragmented into rival blocs. A measure of the distribution of international flows across partner economies suggests that trends that were typical of global interconnectedness in 2019 are now back in place. Even so, the future of globalization is still in question.

US–PRC Economic Tensions

Trade and geopolitical tensions between the US and the PRC from 2019 saw the two largest economies raise tariffs and impose restrictions on various goods. The back-and-forth announcement of new tariff measures, which signal a clear manifestation of economic polarization, has weighed down on global growth and forced many economies to adjust their strategies to better position their exporting sectors. As anticipated, a portion of the trade between the US and the PRC—which share the longest trade distance relationship in the world—ended up being redirected to third jurisdictions to avoid the cost of the newly imposed levies. More recently, growing evidence confirms that US and European investment in strategic sectors, from semiconductors to telecommunications and pharmaceutical products, is shifting away from the PRC, while expanding in other economies in the region. These developments could be an early sign of global supply chain reallocation, with potential spillover effects on other economies.

As derisking strategies move forward, the impact on the pace and form of globalization in this new context are yet to be seen. A true decoupling between the US and the PRC would be expected to influence a fragmentation into rival blocs that would impact the level of global integration. Research suggests that whereas such fragmentation would be costly for both blocs, the PRC-aligned bloc might incur deeper negative effects considering that the US-aligned block enjoys a larger share of economic activities (Altman and Bastian 2023).

Global Shocks: COVID-19 and the Russian Invasion of Ukraine

Just as the US-PRC trade tensions seemingly started to fizzle, COVID-19 emerged. The pandemic was an immense negative shock to the global economy. Governments implemented measures, including lockdowns, to control the spread of coronavirus which exposed inadequacies of national health systems and froze economic activity. These put health care systems under considerable strain and disrupted economic activity. The shock was amplified through financial, trade, and global value chain linkages, creating spillovers from one economy to another. Protracted efforts to contain the pandemic caused significant job losses even as the surging use of digital tools managed to keep some industries afloat.

The Russian invasion of Ukraine complicated the policy environment at a time economies were still recovering from COVID-19. The invasion has also proven to be a difficult test for multilateral instruments tasked with ensuring economic and institutional stability. Considering the role of the Russian Federation and Ukraine in the global energy and food trade, inflation quickly gained momentum globally, forcing advanced and developing economies alike to tighten monetary policy. High debt levels and the still-feeble labor sector recovery amid rising interest rates, however, raised the specter of global economic crisis.

Trade and Supply Chain Disruptions

Disruption of the international supply chain was a prominent consequence in all of these developments. Policymakers, especially in advanced economies, gave in for a time to the rise of nationalist sentiment by imposing trade restrictions and export controls on the distribution of essential goods and medical supplies. This put into question the depth of the commitment to open trade. Logistics concerns coupled with protectionist measures ultimately led to difficulties in sourcing inputs, shortages, rising shipping and transportation costs, and security concerns.

Global interconnectedness also implies that the undesirable impacts of disruption, like key commodity shortages, are typically not localized. Their effects usually spill over to companies, sectors, and economies. The pandemic highlighted the need to strengthen supply chain management and introduce major reforms to global supply chains. Depending on their vulnerabilities, economies are trying to balance diversification with reshoring and nearshoring strategies to mitigate risks and enhance resilience (Kang 2022).

1.3 A New Agenda for Inclusive, Resilient, and Sustainable Globalization

Digital Economy as a New Engine

Rapid digitalization is enabling new forms of connectivity, transforming how goods and services are produced, traded, and delivered (ADB 2022a). Geographic borders no longer limit interactions between consumers and businesses and investors and borrowers. The pandemic accelerated digital technologies across wholesale and retail trade, and services in finance, food, logistics, and transportation, to name just a few of the sectors where their use is now more prominent and accepted.

Digital platforms have empowered new business models and global linkages while reducing transaction costs and information asymmetries (ADB 2021c). In parallel, digital services are increasingly used as inputs in production networks, with potential effects to enhance participation in global value chains. As it stands, digitally deliverable services trade in Asia and the Pacific has grown to a size second only to the European Union (EU). And even as global and regional services trade tumbled with the onset of COVID-19, digitally deliverable services were resilient (ADB 2022a).

Concerns have been raised, however, about the implications of digitalization for competition, data privacy, protection for digital platform workers, and taxation (ADB 2021a). Digital rules and regulations are responding to these different priorities, with goals to protect consumer data and privacy and to promote data flows that can be trusted between different jurisdictions. While a balance in catering to these interests is necessary, jurisdictions have different approaches in practice. A regional consensus on key areas such as data privacy, free cross-border data flows, and the protection of national interests is still in the making.

Globalization and Inclusiveness

A key concern about globalization is that fierce competition may contribute to economic and social inequalities between individuals or economies that could generate income and political polarization, undermining social and cultural cohesion. The view of globalization as a force for widening inequality, increasing economic dependence of less developed economies, and undermining sociocultural diversity has intensified (Bourguignon 2016; Milanovic 2016).

Given the concerns related to economic and social inequalities, inclusiveness is becoming a critical ingredient for making globalization meaningful. Technological solutions carry the promise of reaching those at economic peripheries and fostering a more equal landscape for opportunity. That said, without enabling policies, technology can deepen the divides between economic agents in an advantageous position and those that are disadvantaged. Access and affordability are key elements to harness the potential of digital solutions in promoting inclusivity. Good understanding of the characteristics of digital tools is also critical in maintaining, if not strengthening, consumer trust in the ecosystem.

Environmental Sustainability

An equally relevant concern is the impact of globalization on the environment, in particular its contribution to climate change, pollution, and the degradation of natural resources. These issues have negative implications on economic growth and overall well-being. Whereas it is unclear whether global economic integration has a direct incidence on environmental degradation, some linkages have been established. Carbon-intensive industries, such as coal, oil refining, air transport, and electricity supply produce output that is traded more often than the output of non-carbon intensive industries such as real estate and financial services. This suggests that trade does have an impact on the environment (OECD 2013; Copeland, Shapiro, and Taylor 2021).

Awareness of the effects of climate change has given rise to regional and global initiatives to reduce greenhouse gas emissions. One initiative is the adoption of carbon markets, which seek to put a price on carbon emissions either through carbon taxation or an emissions trading system. Such carbon pricing mechanisms can ensure emissions reduction is done at lowest cost (ADB 2023a, 2023b). Yet, carbon pricing mechanisms remain limited and small, both in the number of implementing economies and the sectors covered. To create a global carbon market and meet climate change goals, it is important to broaden the scope of carbon pricing through increased regional integration. International climate cooperation as embodied in the Paris Agreement, Kyoto Protocol, and Copenhagen Accord has been critical to this end.

Global negotiations and incorporating environmental provisions in bilateral or regional trade and investment agreements are important, while trade in environmental goods and services should be further liberalized (ADB 2021b). Global integration has also helped encourage research and the exchange of environmental solutions and green technologies.

1.4   The Need for a Better Measure of Globalization

Capturing the New Global Agenda and Dimensions

The globalization debate is broadening out to include critical yet relatively unexplored issues. Recent trends, from geopolitical tensions, COVID-19, digitalization, and supply chain disruptions, are inevitably linked to the globalization process. Having a clearer picture of the costs and benefits of global integration underscores the importance of having a proper measure of globalization. Using proxies for economic globalization such as trade and capital flows or openness to these flows, is informative, although they do not adequately capture the complex and multifaceted nature of globalization.

The Global Integration Index and Other Measures

Previous studies have focused on developing composite measures that reflect different facets of globalization. The Foreign Policy (2001) was probably the first attempt to build a composite measure of globalization. Several others followed, including the G-Index, CSGR Globalization Index, Maastricht Globalization Index, KOF Index of Globalization, the DHL Global Interconnectedness Index, and the Global Economic Integration Index. Annex 1.1 summarizes these different initiatives. Whereas the indexes differ in economy coverage, time periods, indicators, and methodology, they all combine economy-level information to produce one aggregate measure of globalization.

The Global Integration index (GII) presented in this report builds upon ADB's Asia-Pacific Regional Cooperation and Integration Index (ARCII) and a previous global integration index (Huh and Park 2021). The index has been expanded to improve measurement and better capture the increasingly complex dimensions of globalization. The new framework includes two new dimensions: technology and digital connectivity, and environmental cooperation. The technology and digital connectivity dimension responds to the growing role of digital technologies in deepening globalization. Environmental cooperation, on the other hand, refers to environmental factors with global effects and how economies coordinate policies to address environmental risks. A variety of new indicators are also incorporated in the existing dimensions, including for services trade, value-added, international flight passengers, cultural goods trade, and trademark applications. The framework expands from 25 to 43 indicators, increases the original sample by 15 economies, and includes 4 new years.

Connecting Global and Regional Integration Measures

The report also introduces a Regional Integration Index (RII) compatible with the GII to measure an economy's social and economic exchanges with other economies in the region. This addition helps to assess how economies fare in both regional and global integration on the same footing.

Regional cooperation and integration (RCI) is thought to provide economic opportunities while being less exposed to global competition and the risks of full economic liberalization. Given that RCI is one of seven operational priorities in ADB's Strategy 2030, efforts have been made to track its scale, mode, and pace in Asia and the Pacific. Regional integration has expanded in tandem with rapid globalization, and early on attention was paid to how regionalism related to globalization (Söderbaum and Shaw 2003; Sampson and Woolcock 2003; Drysdale 2017). Recognition that globalization can come with risks has garnered support for so-called open regionalism, a departure from the exclusive, protectionist trading blocs in previous decades.

Under open regionalism, regionalization is regarded as a stepping stone to globalization. Economies can test their products in regional markets, improve liberalization policies, and increase their capacity to integrate into global markets. Economies, particularly small developing ones, may have spearheaded regionalization for economic openness as a strategy to build economic and financial resilience and take a more controlled path toward globalization. An example of open regionalism is embodied in the Association of Southeast Asian Nations (ASEAN). A key component of the ASEAN framework is the elimination of all barriers to regional economic integration while remaining "actively engaged, outward-looking, inclusive and non-discriminatory." ASEAN has moved away from a protectionist policy and encourages members to pursue external economic partnerships to further regional and global integration.

Assessing the Economic and Welfare Effects of Global and Regional Integration

The third part of this study briefly presents empirical results on the effects of global and regional integration on three key development outcomes: economic growth, income inequality, and inclusive growth.

Although the contribution of global and regional economic integration to economic growth is generally acknowledged, the impact on income inequality is more contentious. Evidence suggests that inequality has worsened over the past 3 decades of intensive global integration. The implications of globalization for inclusive growth have also been less explored. This report explores possible channels through which global economic integration impacts these development outcomes, and the contribution of regional integration in this process. It also seeks to offer policymakers useful guidance for shaping and directing their integration policies at global and/ or regional levels.

Chapter 2 briefly explains the construction and main features of the GII and RII. Chapter 3 discusses trends in global and regional economic integration. Chapter 4 examines their effects on development outcomes, including economic growth, income inequality, and inclusive growth. Chapter 5 provides a conclusion on the implications from the GII for the region.

References

Altman, S. and C. Bastian. 2023. *DHL Global Connectedness Index 2022: An In-depth Report on the State of Globalization*. San Francisco: DHL.

Arslan, Y., J. Contreras, N. Patel, and C. Shu. 2018. Globalisation and Deglobalisation in Emerging Market Economies: Facts and Trends. *BIS Papers*. 100a. Basel: Bank for International Settlements.

Asian Development Bank (ADB). 2018. *Asian Economic Integration Report 2018: Toward Optimal Provision of Regional Public Goods in Asia and the Pacific*. Manila.

————. 2021a. *Asian Economic Integration Report 2021: Making Digital Platform Works for Asia and the Pacific*. Manila.

————. 2021b. Asia–Pacific Regional Cooperation and Integration Index: Enhanced Framework, Analysis, and Applications. Manila.

————. 2021c. *Global Value Chain Development Report 2021: Beyond Production*. Manila.

————. 2022a. *Asian Economic Integration Report 2022: Advancing Digital Services Trade in Asia and the Pacific*. Manila.

————. 2022b. *Asian Development Outlook (ADO) 2022 Update: Entrepreneurship in the Digital Age*. Manila.

————. 2023a. *Asian Economic Integration Report: Trade, Investment, and Climate Change*. Manila.

————. 2023b. *Asia Development Outlook 2023 Thematic Report: Asia in the Global Transition to Net Zero*. Manila.

Bourguignon, F. 2016. Inequality and Globalization: How the Rich Get Richer as the Poor Catch Up. *Council on Foreign Relations Foreign Affairs*. 95 (1). pp. 11–15.

Copeland, B. R., J. S. Shapiro, and M. S. Taylor. 2021. Globalization and the Environment. *NBER Working Papers*. 28797. Cambridge, MA: National Bureau of Economic Research.

Dreher, A., Gaston, N., and P. Martens. 2008. *Measuring Globalisation: Gauging its Consequences*. New York: Springer.

Drysdale, P. 2017. *ASEAN: The Experiment in Open Regionalism that Exceeded*. https://www.eria.org/5.1.ASEAN_50_Vol_5_Drysdale.pdf.

Figge, L. and, P. Martens. 2014. Globalisation Continues: The Maastricht Globalisation Index Revisited and Updated. *Globalizations*. 11. pp. 875–893.

Foreign Policy. 2001. Measuring Globalization. 2001. No. 122. pp. 56–65. https://doi.org/10.2307/3183226. 2001. Measuring Globalization. *Foreign Policy*. 122. pp. 56–65.

Gygli, S., F. Haelg, and J-E. Sturm. 2018. The KOF Globalization Index - Revisited. *KOF Working Paper.* No. 439. KOF Swiss Economic Institute.

Huh, H. S. and C. Y. Park. 2021. A New Index of Globalization: Measuring Impacts of Integration on Economic Growth and Income Inequality. *The World Economy.* 44 (2). pp. 409–43.

International Monetary Fund (IMF). 2022a. *World Economic Outlook: Gloomy and More Uncertain.* Washington, DC.

———. 2022b. *World Economic Outlook: War Sets Back the Global Recovery.* Washington, DC.

Kang, J. W. 2022. Reshore or Diversify? How to Reorganize the World's Fragile Supply Chains. *Asian Development Blog.* 3 August. https://blogs.adb.org/blog/how-to-reorganize-the-world-s-fragile-supply-chains.

Lockwood, B. and M. Redoano. 2005. The CSGR Globalization Index: An Introductory Guide. *Center for the Study of Globalisation and Regionalisation Working Paper.* No. 155/04. University of Warwick.

Martens, P. and D. Zywietz. 2006. Rethinking Globalization: A Modified Globalization Index. *Journal of International Economics.* 18. pp. 331–350.

Milavonic, B. 2016. *Global Inequality: A New Approach for the Age of Globalization.* Cambridge, MA: Belknap Press.

Randolph, J. 2001. *G-Index: Globalization Measured.* London: World Markets Research Centre.

Sampson, G. and S. Woolcock. 2003. *Regionalism, Multilateralism and Economic Integration: The Recent Experience.* Tokyo: United Nations University Press.

Soderbaum F. and T. Shaw. 2003. *Theories of New Regionalism.* London: Palgrave MacMIllan.

Organisation for Economic Co-operation and Development (OECD). 2013. What Is the Impact of Globalization on the Environment? In OECD. *Economic Globalization: Origins and Consequences.* Paris: OECD Publishing.

World Trade Organization (WTO), 2022. *World Trade Report 2022—Climate Change and Trade.* Geneva.

Annex 1.1: Review of Composite Measures of Globalization

Author/s (Year)	Name	Dimensions	Coverage	Method
Foreign Policy (2001)	Magazine Globalization Index	14 indicators under 4 dimensions (economic integration, personal contact, technology, and political engagement)	62 economies	Panel min-max normalization (based on all sample years and economies). Index scores for each economy and year are derived by summing the scores across panels (giving double weights for more important indicators)
Randolph (2001)	G-Index	3 dimensions (90% economics, 5% telephone traffic, 5% internet hosts)	185 economies	
Lockwood and Redoano (2005)	CSGR Globalization Index	16 indicators under 3 subindexes (economic globalization, social globalization, political globalization)	Around 200 economies; 1970–2001	Panel min-max normalization (based on all sample years and economies); Principal component analysis for weighting
Martens and Zywietz 2006; Figge and Martens 2014	Maastricht Globalization Index (updated version)	11 indicators under 5 domains (political, economic, social and cultural, technological, and environmental)	117 economies; 2000, 2008, 2012	Logarithmic transformation of indicators with skewed distributions; Equal weighting is applied in both aggregation steps
Dreher et al. 2008; Gygli, Haelg, and Sturm 2018	KOF Globalization Index (2018 Version)	43 indicators under 3 dimensions (economic, social, and political; distinguishing between de facto and de jure)	203 economies; 1970–2016	Panel min-max normalization (based on all sample years and economies); Principal component analysis for weighting; Aggregation by adding up individual weighted variables
Huh and Park (2021)	Global Integration Index (2021)	25 indicators under 6 dimensions (trade and investment, money and finance, value chain, infrastructure and connectivity, movement of people, institutional and social integration)	158 economies; 2006–2014	Z-score standardization; Principal component analysis for weighting
Altman and Bastian (2023)	DHL Global Interconnectedness Index	Measures the depth and breadth of international flows of trade, capital, information, and people flows relative to domestic activity and geographic reach, using bilateral flows	2001 to 2021	Panel normalization; Weights based on subjective judgment on the relative importance of components to globalization

continued on next page

Annex 1.1 *continued*

Author/s (Year)	Name	Dimensions	Coverage	Method
ADB	Global Integration Index (2022)	43 indicators under 8 dimensions (trade and investment integration, money and finance integration, global value chain, infrastructure and connectivity, people and social integration, institutional arrangements, technology and digital connectivity, and environment)	173 economies; 2006–2021	Panel min-max normalization (based on all sample years and economies); Principal component analysis for weighting

Sources: ADB compilation based on Altman and Bastian (2023); Dreher, Gaston, and Martens (2008); Figge and Martens (2014); Foreign Policy (2002); Gygli, Haelg, and Sturm (2018); Huh and Park (2021); Lockwood and Redoano (2005); Martens and Zywietz (2006); and Randolph (2001).

Global Integration Index Construction and Trends

2.1 Introduction: Building a New Framework

The Global Integration Index (GII) is a multidimensional measure of global integration. It was initially developed in 2021 and introduced as the Global Economic Integration Index (GEII). The new GII is constructed alongside the Regional Integration Index (RII). In comparison to examining global integration and regional integration separately, a similar structure enables the use of the GII and RII to consider interactions between global and regional linkages. Finding compatible frameworks between global and regional integration indexes was an important motivation for this report. This chapter elaborates on the framework and methodology used to construct the GII and RII estimates. It also presents the main trends in global integration identified in the GII, while Chapter 3 provides an overview of regional integration based on the RII.

The new GII consists of 43 indicators that measure different aspects of globalization, classified into eight dimensions, with technology and digital connectivity, and environmental cooperation expanding the list of six dimensions in the original framework by Huh and Park (2021). The eight dimensions covered by the index are trade and investment, money and finance, global value chain, infrastructure and connectivity, people and social integration, institutional arrangements, technology and digital connectivity, and environmental cooperation.

Improvements in Scope and Measurement

The new dimension for technology and digital connectivity reflects its growing role in economic activity. Digital technologies have been essential for deepening globalization by changing how firms and individuals participate in trade, cross-border production networks, and social exchanges. The growing presence of digital platforms has led to faster cross-border communications and transactions at lower cost. These have enabled more stakeholders, such as small businesses, to tap global markets and helped facilitate technological transfer and innovation (ADB 2020, 2021b, 2022c).

Environmental cooperation, on the other hand, is seldom considered in multidimensional measures of globalization. One exception is the Maastricht Globalization Index by Figge and Martens (2014), which considers an indicator of the ecological footprint of trade as a share of biocapacity. One reason for this absence is the thinking that environmental factors are consequences of globalization rather than separate driving forces. However, as Dreher, Gaston, and Martens (2008) point out, environmental factors can eventually become driving forces. While some environmental issues—such as water pollution or soil degradation—remain local, they increasingly have regional and global effects. Therefore, coordination and cooperation are needed on plurilateral climate mitigation and adaptation policies, policies that can promote interconnectedness across economies and enhance environmental sustainability, which is core to the United Nations 2030 Agenda for Sustainable Development.

The Regional Integration Index (RII) is based on the same structure as the Global Integration Index, which ensures compatibility between the two indexes. While closely associated in structure and scope, the definitions of indicators of the RII and ADB's Asia-Pacific Regional Cooperation and Integration Index (ARCII) are slightly different. Most differences stem from the use of alternative denominators (i.e., gross domestic product, population). Table 2.1 presents the GII and RII indicators by dimension as well as their data sources. A more detailed description of the indicators can be found in the *Asia-Pacific Regional Cooperation and Integration Index: Enhanced Framework, Analysis and Applications* report (ADB 2021a).[1] Box 2.1 provides examples on new indicators included in the framework.

The GII covers 173 economies across six regions from 2006 to 2021: Asia and the Pacific, the European Union (EU), Latin America, Africa, Middle East, and North America. Annex 2.1 provides a list of economies covered by the index.

Table 2.1: Global (Regional) Integration Index: Dimensions and Indicators

Pillar		Indicator	Data Source
P1. Trade and Investment Integration (6)	P1a	Ratio of total (regional) goods exports to GDP	IMF Direction of Trade, World Bank World Development Indicators
	P1b	Ratio of total (regional) goods imports to GDP	IMF Direction of Trade, World Bank World Development Indicators
	P1c	Ratio of total services exports to GDP	WTO Trade in Services annual data set
	P1d	Ratio of total services imports to GDP	WTO Trade in Services annual data set
	P1e	Ratio of total (regional) FDI inflows to GDP	fDi Markets Greenfield FDI, Zephyr M&A FDI
	P1f	Ratio of total (regional) FDI inflows plus outflows to GDP	fDi Markets Greenfield FDI, Zephyr M&A FDI
P2. Money and Finance Integration (5)	P2a	Ratio of total (regional) cross-border equity liabilities to GDP	IMF Coordinated Portfolio Investment Survey
	P2b	Ratio of total (regional) cross-border bond liabilities to GDP	IMF Coordinated Portfolio Investment Survey
	P2c	Pair-wise dispersion of deposit rates averaged over all (regional) trading partners	CEIC Data Company and Haver Analytics
	P2d*	Capital account openness	Chinn-Ito Index (Chinn and Ito 2006)
	P2e	Correlations of exchange rates against the US dollar, averaged over all (regional) trading partners	CEIC Data Company and Haver Analytics
P3. Global (Regional) Value Chain (5)	P3a	Averaged trade complementarity index over all (regional) trading partners	UN Commodity Trade Database
	P3b	Averaged trade concentration index over all (regional) trading partners	UN Commodity Trade Database
	P3c	Ratio of total (regional) intermediate goods exports to total (regional) goods exports	UN Commodity Trade Database

continued on next page

---

[1] A notable exception would be the indicator on CO_2 emissions (P8c), which is neither contained in the baseline globalization index and enhanced ARCII framework.

Table 2.1 *continued*

Pillar		Indicator	Data Source
	P3d	Ratio of total (regional) intermediate goods imports to total (regional) goods imports	UN Commodity Trade Database
	P3e	Ratio of the sum of the value-added contributed by all (regional) trading partners to total (regional) exports	UNCTAD-Eora Global Value Chain Database
P4. Infrastructure and Connectivity (5)	P4a	Averaged trade cost over all (regional) trading partners	ESCAP-World Bank Trade Cost Database
	P4b	Averaged liner shipping connectivity index over all (regional) trading partners	UNCTADStat
	P4c	Ratio of passenger seats sold on all (regional) flights to population	ICAO Passenger Traffic by City Pair Data
	P4d*	Logistics performance index	World Bank
	P4e*	Doing Business Index	World Bank
P5. People and Social Integration (6)	P5a	Ratio of total (regional) outbound migration to population	United Nations Population Division, World Bank World Development Indicators
	P5b	Ratio of total (regional) tourists inbound plus outbound to population	UN World Tourism Organization Tourism Dashboard
	P5c	Ratio of total (regional) remittances to GDP	World Bank World Development Indicators
	P5d	Cultural proximity averaged over all (regional) trading partners	CEPII Gravity Database
	P5e	Ratio of total (regional) cultural goods exports plus imports to GDP	UN Commodity Trade Database
	P5f	Ratio of trademark applications made with foreign (regional) residents to the population	WIPO IP Statistics Data Center
P6. Institutional Arrangements (5)	P6a	Ratio of all (regional) trading partners that have signed FTAs with	Design of Trade Agreements Database (Dür, Baccini, and Elsig 2014)
	P6b	Ratio of all (regional) trading partners that have signed business investment treaties with	UNCTAD International Investment Agreements Navigator
	P6c	Ratio of all (regional) trading partners that have signed double taxation treaties with	UNCTAD, IBFD
	P6d*	Number of international intergovernment organizations joined	CIA The World Factbook
	P6e	Ratio of all (regional) trading partners that have an embassy	Europa World Yearbook
P7. Technology and Digital Connectivity (6)	P7a	Ratio of all (regional) ICT goods exports and imports to GDP	UN Commodity Trade Database
	P7b	Ratio of research outputs with foreign (regional) collaborators to population	Clarivate Web of Science

continued on next page

Table 2.1 *continued*

Pillar		Indicator	Data Source
	P7c	Ratio of patent applications made with foreign (regional) residents to total patents applications	WIPO IP Statistics Data Center
	P7d*	Ratio of persons using the internet to population	ITU ICT data
	P7e*	Mobile subscriptions per 100 persons	ITU ICT data
	P7f*	International internet bandwidth per internet user	ITU ICT data
P8. Environment (5)	P8a	Ratio of total (regional) environmental goods exports and imports to total (regional) goods export and imports	UN Commodity Trade Database
	P8b*	Number of international environmental agreements ratified	CIA The World Factbook
	P8c*	CO_2 emissions per capita	Global Carbon Budget (Friedlingstein et al. 2022)
	P8d*	Ecological footprint of consumption per capita minus biocapacity per capita	Global Footprint Network

CIA = Central Intelligence Agency, CEPII = Centre d'Etudes Prospectives et d'Informations Internationales, FDI = foreign direct investment, FTA = free trade agreement, GDP = gross domestic product, IBFD = International Bureau of Fiscal Documentation, ICT = information and communication technology, IMF = International Monetary Fund, IP = intellectual property, ITU = International Telecommunications Union, M&A = merger and acquisition, UN = United Nations, UNCTAD = United Nations Conference on Trade and Development, WIPO = World Intellectual Property Organization.

Notes: In the indicator column, cases for the Regional Integration Index are in parentheses. Highlighted rows in green indicate new indicators and dimensions included in comparison with Huh, H. S, and C. Y. Park. 2021. A New Index of Globalization: Measuring Impacts of Integration on Economic Growth and Income Inequality. *The World Economy*. 44 (2). pp. 409–43. Indicators marked with asterisks are national-level indicators.

Source: Asian Development Bank compilation.

Box 2.1: New Indicators in the Global Integration Index: Examples

Indicators presented here correspond to new items that are not included the baseline Global Economic Integration Index in Huh and Park (2021) or in ADB's Asia-Pacific Regional Cooperation and Integration Index. The description in this box provides a basic rationale on how these concepts are related to global and regional integration.

Carbon emissions

The emission of carbon dioxide (CO_2) is considered one of the largest contributing factors to climate change. Global CO_2 emissions are increasing, and Asia and the Pacific accounts for around half the global total, while North America and the Middle East have the highest per capita CO_2 emissions. Regional and global efforts to reduce CO_2 emissions are critical to tackling climate change. The Paris Agreement at the Conference of the Parties, which include commitments to limit global warming below 2°C, is particularly important.

The link between global integration and CO_2 emissions is complex. No full consensus exists on their nexus and mutual implications. By encouraging economic activity, globalization contributes to higher carbon releases. At the same time, globalization increases technological spillovers, the adoption of green technologies, and awareness to adopt greener production methods. The Global Integration Index (GII) includes an indicator on CO_2 emissions per capita to capture the emissions trend (Figure 2.1.1).

Figure 2.1.1: Per Capita Carbon Dioxide Emissions by Region
(tonnes per capita)

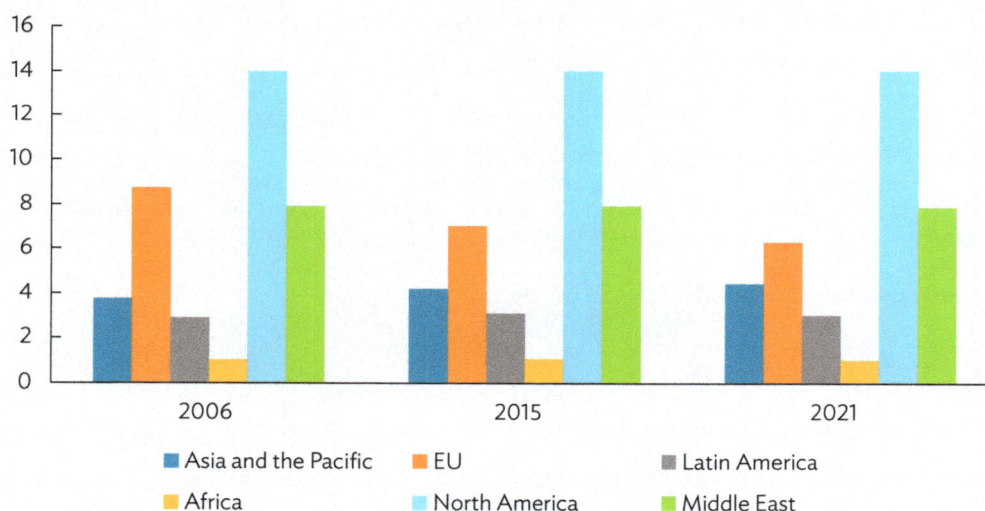

EU = European Union.

Source: ADB calculations using data from Friedlingstein et al. 2022. Global Carbon Budget 2022. *Earth System Science Data*. 14 (11). pp. 4811–4900. https://doi.org/10.5194/essd-14-4811-2022 (accessed May 2023).

continued on next page

Box 2.1 *continued*

Services trade

Services, from transportation to finance, telecommunications, and intellectual property, play a major role in international trade and economic development (Figure 2.1.2). They are important inputs in production and trade. Services have also become more tradable as digitalization and advancements in technology continue to open new avenues for their cross-border trade (Molinuevo and Sáez 2014; ADB 2022). A globalized services market could bring about fuller economic integration, promote global competition, and augment economic growth (WTO 2019). Two indicators on the ratio of total services exports to GDP (P1c) and total services imports to GDP (P1d) are incorporated in the GII. As of 2021, services trade exports accounted for 6.3% of global GDP and 21.4% of total trade in goods and services (UNCTAD 2022).

Figure 2.1.2: Trade in Services Exports by Region (% GDP)

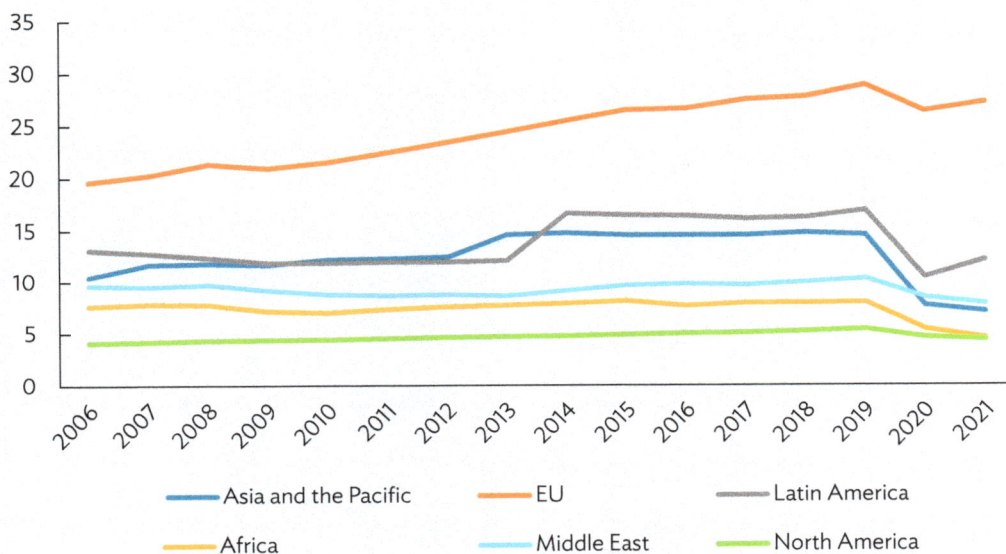

EU = European Union.

Source: ADB calculations using data from WTO. Trade in Services Annual Data Set. http://stats.wto.org/assets/UserGuide/services_annual_dataset.zip; World Bank. World Development Indicators. https://databank.worldbank.org/source/world-developmentindicators (all accessed November 2023).

2.2 Methodology

For both the Global Integration Index and the Regional Integration Index, construction involves six main steps (Figure 2.1). The first step takes in data collection and imputation of missing data. After the data set is assembled, indicators are normalized to standardize their units. After normalization, the indicators are weighted and aggregated to produce the global (regional) integration index, with the weights computed using a principal components analysis (PCA) approach.

The PCA groups collinear indicators to form a composite index that can capture as much common information as possible.[2] Results from the PCA indicate that significantly fewer principal components than the maximum number are chosen, while accounting for a large share of the total variation in the indicators (Annex 2.2). The obtained weights are also different from equal weighting, sometimes used in other composite indexes. A visualization of the steps for index construction is provided in Figure 2.1, with elaboration in Box 2.2.

Figure 2.1: Steps in the Construction of the Global Integration Index

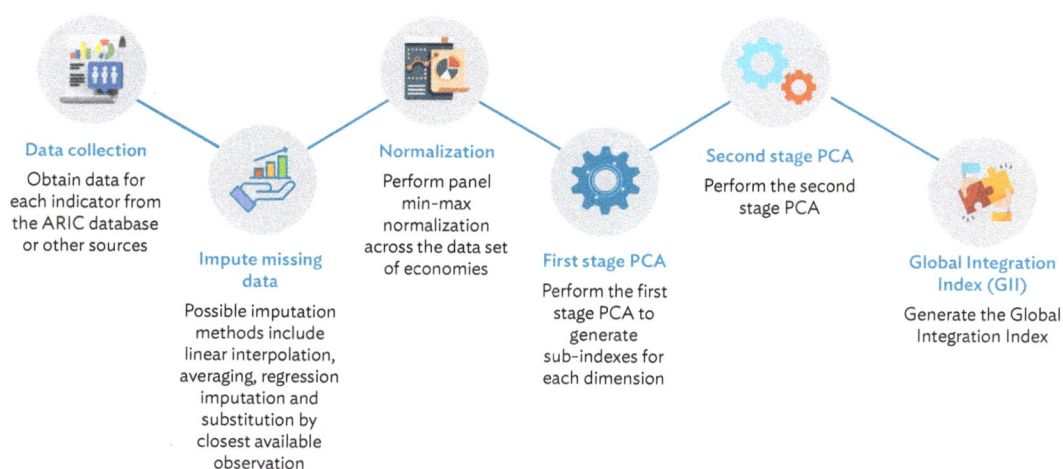

Data collection
Obtain data for each indicator from the ARIC database or other sources

Impute missing data
Possible imputation methods include linear interpolation, averaging, regression imputation and substitution by closest available observation

Normalization
Perform panel min-max normalization across the data set of economies

First stage PCA
Perform the first stage PCA to generate sub-indexes for each dimension

Second stage PCA
Perform the second stage PCA

Global Integration Index (GII)
Generate the Global Integration Index

ARIC = Asia Regional Integration Center, PCA = principal components analysis.
Source: Asian Development Bank.

Index Contributions by Dimension and Indicator

The dimensions and indicators of the GII aim to capture the drivers of global integration. Dimensional contributions in Asia and the Pacific appear broadly balanced when compared to other regions, and its main driver toward global integration is the environment dimension (Figure 2.2a). Overall, dimensional contributions in the EU are similar to Asia and the Pacific, although technology and digital connectivity contribute more to the EU's global integration. For Latin America and Africa, the environment dimension reported the highest contributions; this dimension alone explains about 20% of global integration in these regions. In almost all regions, trade and investment integration and people and social integration have lower contributions than the other dimensions.

---

[2]   Indicators are given equal weight when choosing the maximum number of principal components (i.e., the total number of indicators) corresponding to the case of using all correlations in the data—choosing less than the maximum number of principal components serves to trim off the least common (or equivalently, the most distinctive) movements in the indicators. In PCA, the extent to which the least common movements are discarded can be monitored according to the selection of the principal components.

Box 2.2: Principal Components Analysis and Its Application to Integration Indexes

Principal components analysis (PCA) is a widely used statistical technique for creating composite indexes. The procedure is appropriate when the components measure different aspects of a composite index (Gwartney and Lawson 2001). It is a useful tool among existing weighting schemes, especially when each dimension has a small number of indicators (OECD 2008). Other studies have adopted PCA to combine sets of indicators into single composites. Examples include the KOF Index of Globalization (KOF Swiss Economic Institute), Economic Freedom of the World Index (Fraser Institute), Chicago Fed National Activity Index (Federal Reserve Bank of Chicago), and the General Indicator of Science and Technology (National Institute of Science and Technology Policy).

The Global Integration Index (GII) framework applies the PCA to synthesize the indicators that capture the different elements of global and regional integration. A brief background on the steps implemented to generate the GII through the PCA is provided below.

Data Collection and Imputation

Historical data are collected to compute for the indicators, based on descriptions provided in Table 2.2 of this chapter. These data are updated annually. Most indicators are based on bilateral (economy-to-economy) data, and only a few are based on national level data.

Data availability is a prevalent issue when working with high geographic coverage and multiple indicators. In the case of the GII and RII, data for some indicators are not available for all economies or across the full time period. In principle, dimensional indexes and the overall index are not computed for economies with missing data. For some cases, however, this is addressed to secure a minimum number of economies for calculation of the composite indexes. Different imputation methods are utilized to fill the data gaps. These include linear interpolation, averaging, regression imputation, and substitution by the closest available observation.

Normalization

As measurement units can differ between indicators, normalization prior to aggregation is required to bring these indicators to the same standard. Among the normalization methods, panel min-max scheme is widely used in most composite indexes. Examples include the Human Development Index (UNDP), Doing Business Index (World Bank), KOF Index of Globalization (KOF Swiss Economic Institute), and the Economic Freedom of the World Index (Economic Freedom Network). This scheme normalizes indicators in the range of zero to one, based on all sample years and all economies at hand. It is suitable for comparing progress across different economies over time. Higher values denote greater global (regional) integration. To illustrate, the normalized indicator given as X_{ij}^t could be computed with the following formula:

$$X_{ij}^t = \frac{Y_{ij}^t - Y_{i,max}}{Y_{i,max} - Y_{i,min}}$$

Where Y_{ij}^t is the original indicator i for economy j in year t and $Y_{i,max}$ and $Y_{i,min}$ are the maximum and minimum values of indicator I across economies and years. Several cases exist in which higher values of the original indicator imply lower levels of global (regional) integration: deposit rates (P2c), trade concentration index (P3b), trade cost (P4a), CO_2 emissions (P8c), and ecological footprint (P8d). For these indicators, the formula is converted to preserve the ordinal relationship as follows:

$$X_{ij}^t = 1 - \frac{Y_{ij}^t - Y_{i,max}}{Y_{i,max} - Y_{i,min}}$$

continued on next page

Box 2.2 *continued*

Weighting and Aggregation

Once normalized, the indicators are weighted and aggregated to produce the global (regional) integration index in two steps. First, the weighted average of the normalized indicators per dimension are generated to construct the dimensional indexes. Second, the weighted average of the dimensional indexes are used to derive the overall index of global integration.

The weights applied to the indicators and dimensions are empirically determined based on the PCA technique, which can group collinear indicators to form a composite index that captures as much common information as possible. Two main criteria are followed in selecting the number of principal components to be retained for generating the weights: (i) the Kaiser criterion which indicates the selection of components with associated eigenvalues exceeding one; and (ii) the Joliffe criterion, which admits principal components with eigenvalues over 0.7 for cases in which the set of principal components chosen by the Kaiser criterion accounts for an insufficient portion of the variation.

Figure 2.2.1 provides an illustration of how the weight is derived for one indicator. A more detailed account of the methodology for weight computation can be found in Huh and Park (2021) and Park and Claveria (2019).

Figure 2.2.1: Steps in the Construction of Weights

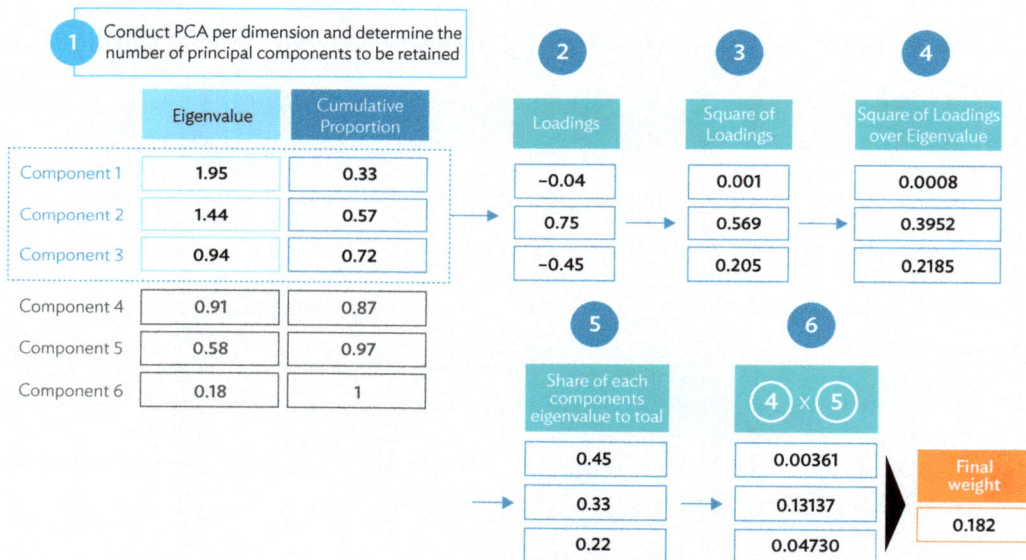

PCA = principal components analysis.

Notes: The PCA is a well-known statistical technique that in this report is employed to determine the weights of each indicator and dimension to create the composite indexes (the Global Integration Index and Regional Integration Index). The PCA partitions the variance in a set of variables and uses it to determine weights that maximize the resulting principal component's variation. In effect, the derived principal component is a linear combination of the original indicators. It captures variations in data to the maximum extent possible. The variance of each principal component is the eigenvalue. The correlation coefficients between the orginal variables and principal components are called loadings. The process above described the way that each of these information are used to derive the final weights.

Source: Asian Development Bank.

Figure 2.2: Dimensional Contributions by Region (%)

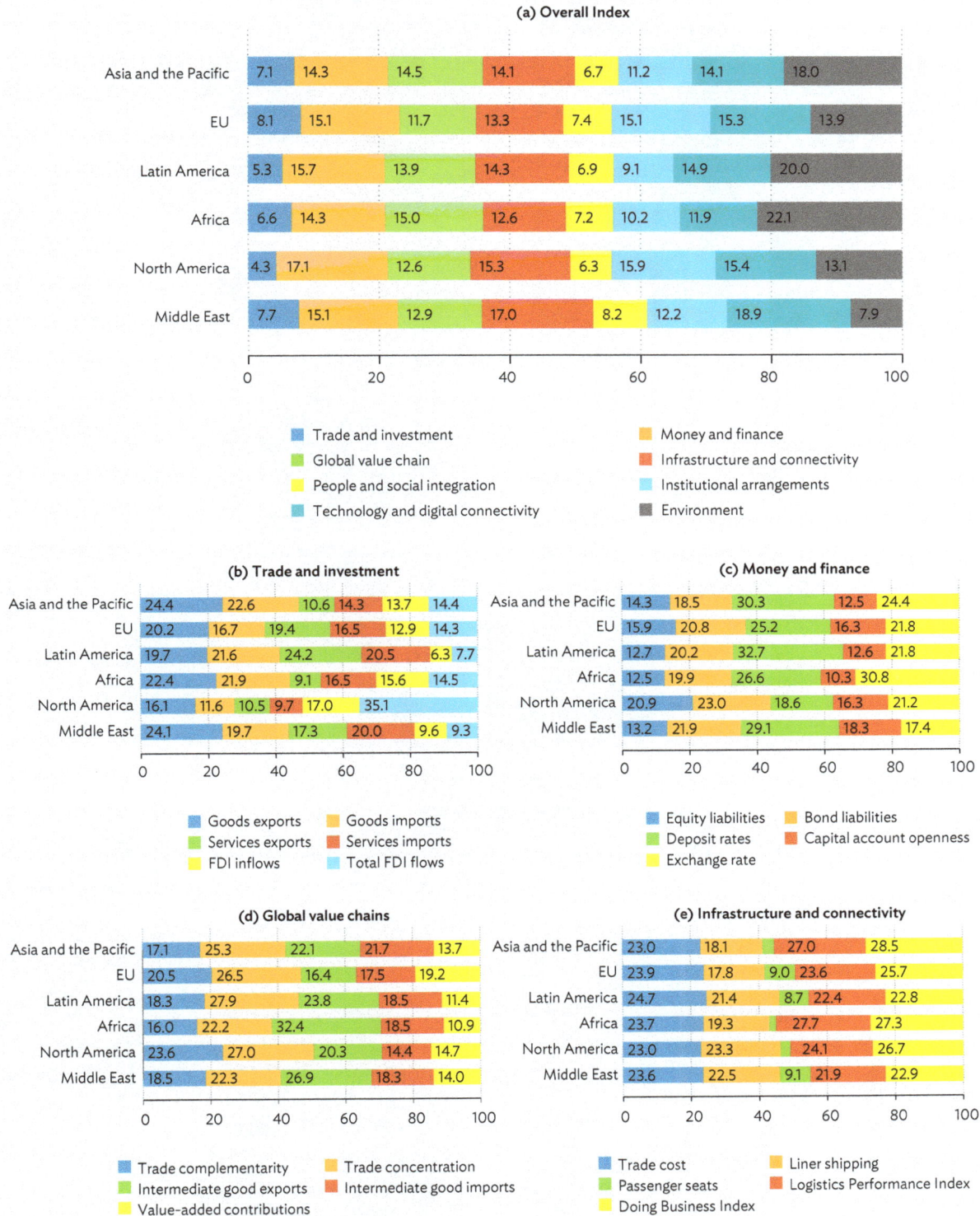

(a) Overall Index

Region	Trade and investment	Money and finance	Global value chain	Infrastructure and connectivity	People and social integration	Institutional arrangements	Technology and digital connectivity	Environment
Asia and the Pacific	7.1	14.3	14.5	14.1	6.7	11.2	14.1	18.0
EU	8.1	15.1	11.7	13.3	7.4	15.1	15.3	13.9
Latin America	5.3	15.7	13.9	14.3	6.9	9.1	14.9	20.0
Africa	6.6	14.3	15.0	12.6	7.2	10.2	11.9	22.1
North America	4.3	17.1	12.6	15.3	6.3	15.9	15.4	13.1
Middle East	7.7	15.1	12.9	17.0	8.2	12.2	18.9	7.9

(b) Trade and investment

Region	Goods exports	Goods imports	Services exports	Services imports	FDI inflows	Total FDI flows
Asia and the Pacific	24.4	22.6	10.6	14.3	13.7	14.4
EU	20.2	16.7	19.4	16.5	12.9	14.3
Latin America	19.7	21.6	24.2	20.5	6.3	7.7
Africa	22.4	21.9	9.1	16.5	15.6	14.5
North America	16.1	11.6	10.5	9.7	17.0	35.1
Middle East	24.1	19.7	17.3	20.0	9.6	9.3

(c) Money and finance

Region	Equity liabilities	Bond liabilities	Deposit rates	Capital account openness	Exchange rate
Asia and the Pacific	14.3	18.5	30.3	12.5	24.4
EU	15.9	20.8	25.2	16.3	21.8
Latin America	12.7	20.2	32.7	12.6	21.8
Africa	12.5	19.9	26.6	10.3	30.8
North America	20.9	23.0	18.6	16.3	21.2
Middle East	13.2	21.9	29.1	18.3	17.4

(d) Global value chains

Region	Trade complementarity	Trade concentration	Intermediate good exports	Intermediate good imports	Value-added contributions
Asia and the Pacific	17.1	25.3	22.1	21.7	13.7
EU	20.5	26.5	16.4	17.5	19.2
Latin America	18.3	27.9	23.8	18.5	11.4
Africa	16.0	22.2	32.4	18.5	10.9
North America	23.6	27.0	20.3	14.4	14.7
Middle East	18.5	22.3	26.9	18.3	14.0

(e) Infrastructure and connectivity

Region	Trade cost	Liner shipping	Passenger seats	Logistics Performance Index	Doing Business Index
Asia and the Pacific	23.0	18.1	27.0	28.5	
EU	23.9	17.8	9.0	23.6	25.7
Latin America	24.7	21.4	8.7	22.4	22.8
Africa	23.7	19.3	27.7	27.3	
North America	23.0	23.3	24.1	26.7	
Middle East	23.6	22.5	9.1	21.9	22.9

continued on next page

Figure 2.2 *continued*

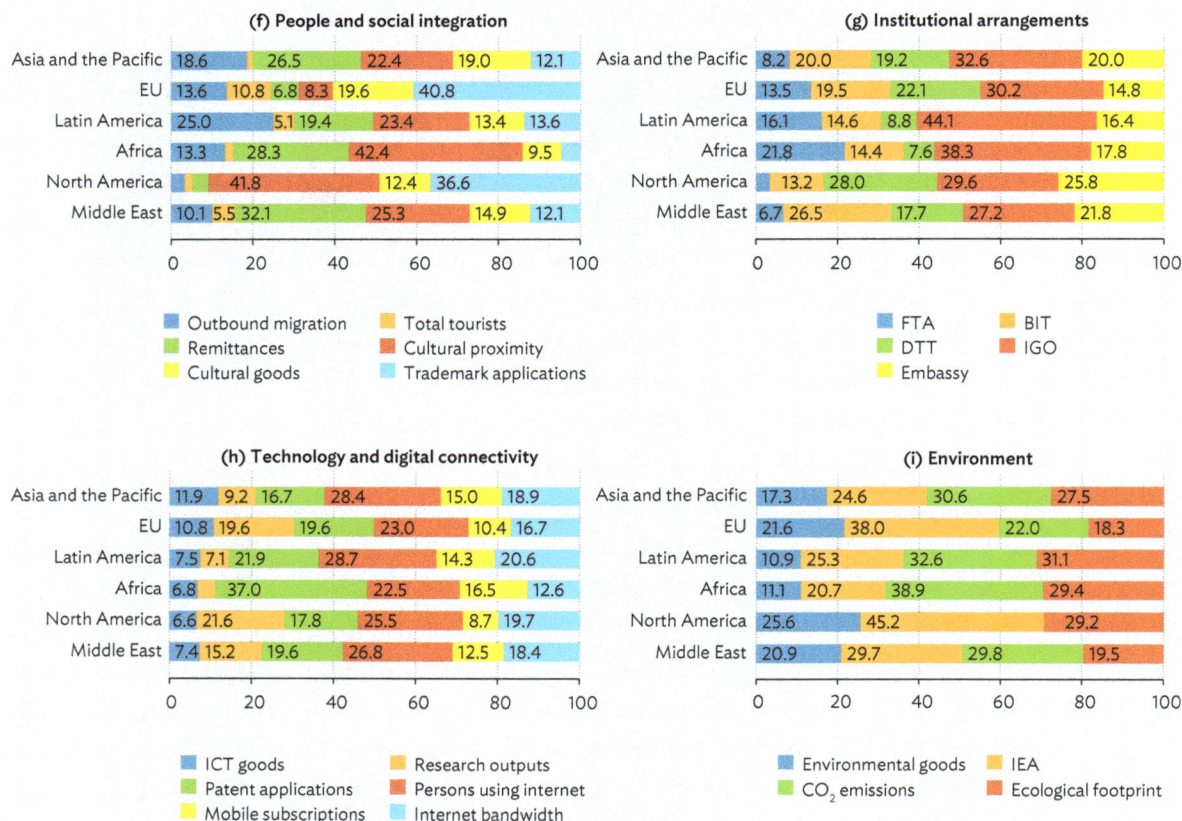

(f) People and social integration

Asia and the Pacific	18.6	26.5	22.4	19.0	12.1	
EU	13.6	10.8	6.8 8.3 19.6	40.8		
Latin America	25.0	5.1 19.4	23.4	13.4	13.6	
Africa	13.3	28.3	42.4	9.5		
North America		41.8	12.4	36.6		
Middle East	10.1 5.5 32.1	25.3	14.9	12.1		

(scale 0 20 40 60 80 100)

- ■ Outbound migration
- ■ Remittances
- ■ Cultural goods
- ■ Total tourists
- ■ Cultural proximity
- ■ Trademark applications

(g) Institutional arrangements

Asia and the Pacific	8.2 20.0	19.2	32.6	20.0	
EU	13.5	19.5	22.1	30.2	14.8
Latin America	16.1	14.6 8.8	44.1	16.4	
Africa	21.8	14.4 7.6	38.3	17.8	
North America	13.2	28.0	29.6	25.8	
Middle East	6.7 26.5	17.7	27.2	21.8	

(scale 0 20 40 60 80 100)

- ■ FTA
- ■ DTT
- ■ Embassy
- ■ BIT
- ■ IGO

(h) Technology and digital connectivity

Asia and the Pacific	11.9	9.2 16.7	28.4	15.0	18.9	
EU	10.8	19.6	19.6	23.0	10.4 16.7	
Latin America	7.5 7.1 21.9	28.7	14.3	20.6		
Africa	6.8	37.0	22.5	16.5	12.6	
North America	6.6 21.6	17.8	25.5	8.7 19.7		
Middle East	7.4 15.2	19.6	26.8	12.5	18.4	

(scale 0 20 40 60 80 100)

- ■ ICT goods
- ■ Patent applications
- ■ Mobile subscriptions
- ■ Research outputs
- ■ Persons using internet
- ■ Internet bandwidth

(i) Environment

Asia and the Pacific	17.3	24.6	30.6	27.5
EU	21.6	38.0	22.0	18.3
Latin America	10.9 25.3	32.6	31.1	
Africa	11.1 20.7	38.9	29.4	
North America	25.6	45.2	29.2	
Middle East	20.9	29.7	29.8	19.5

(scale 0 20 40 60 80 100)

- ■ Environmental goods
- ■ CO_2 emissions
- ■ IEA
- ■ Ecological footprint

BIT = bilateral investment treaty, DTT = double taxation treaty, EU = European Union, FDI = foreign direct investment, ICT = information and communication technology, IEA = international environmental agreement, IGO = intergovernmental organization, FTA = free trade agreement.

Notes: Dimensional contributions represent the product between normalized indicator values and the PCA-derived weights. Therefore, the dimensional indexes are equal to the weighted average of the indicator contributions, while the overall index is equal to the weighted average of the dimensional contributions. The chart above represents these contributions in percentage terms.

Source: ADB calculations using data from ADB. Asia-Pacific Regional Cooperation and Integration Index Database. https://aric.adb.org/database/arcii (accessed November 2023).

For Asia and the Pacific and the EU, contributions in the trade and investment dimension show a similar distribution across indicators. This may imply that goods trade, services trade, and FDI play equally important roles in sustaining trade and investment integration in these regions. Except in North America, for money and finance the indicators on bond liabilities, deposit rates, and exchange rate co-movements mostly explain integration in this dimension across regions. Meanwhile, contributions in the global value chains dimension tend to be skewed in favor of trade complementarity and trade concentration.

For infrastructure and connectivity, the indicator on passenger seat capacity has lower contributions than other indicators in this dimension. Indicator contributions are more diverse in the people and social integration dimension, while Intergovernmental organizations have the largest contribution to institutional integration in most regions, explaining almost one-third of the variation in this dimension. For technology and digital connectivity, mobile subscriptions appear to be less important in explaining digital integration. Finally, indicator contributions in the environment dimension are balanced, except for in Latin America and Africa, where the contribution of environmental goods is lower than for other indicators.

2.3 Comparing GII with the Six-Dimensional Global Economic Integration Index

The Global Integration Index (GII) aims to better capture the increasingly complex dimensions of globalization. As well as adding the two new dimensions (technology and digital connectivity, and the environment), new indicators have been included in existing areas of the six-dimensional baseline. The infrastructure and connectivity dimension now includes indicators on services trade, value-added, international flight passengers, cultural goods trade, and trademark applications. Expansion from 25 to 43 indicators also means that the GII offers a larger scope than other peer indexes. Finally, 15 new economies from the Middle East region are included, bringing the number of economies covered to 173. Table 2.2 compares the main features of the previous and new global integration index.

Table 2.2: Comparison between the Baseline and New Globalization Index

	GEII (IEII): Huh and Park (2021)	GII (RII)
Economy coverage	• 5 regions (Asia and the Pacific, EU, Latin America, Africa, and North America) • 158 economies	• 6 regions (Asia and the Pacific, EU, Latin America, Africa, and North America, and the Middle East) • 173 economies
Dimension and indicator coverage	• 6 dimensions • 25 indicators	• 8 dimensions • 43 indicators (GII)
Normalization method	• Z-score normalization	• Panel min-max normalization
Methodology	• PCA conducted for the intraregional economic integration index (IEII) and the extraregional economic integration index (EEII) • IEII and EEII average to derive the GEII	• PCA conducted for Global Integration Index (GII) and Regional Integration Index (RII) • No corresponding computation for an index measuring extraregional integration

EU = European Union, PCA = principal components analysis.

Source: Huh, H. S. and C. Y. Park. 2021. A New Index of Globalization: Measuring Impacts of Integration on Economic Growth and Income Inequality. *The World Economy.* 44 (2). pp. 409–43.

Trends between the baseline and new global integration indexes are largely consistent (Figure 2.3). Differences between the two indexes, especially at the dimensional level (Figure 2.4), are mainly explained by change in the indicator composition, the normalization method, and the increase in economy coverage in the new framework. Both baseline and new estimates report a dip in 2009 and 2012, although the dip is more accentuated in the baseline GII. By region, North America and the EU show the deepest global integration in both frameworks, while Africa is the least integrated region. Economies in Asia and the Pacific report average levels of global integration (Figure 2.3b). Figure 2.5 confirms the high positive correlation of dimensional indexes in the baseline and new global integration indexes, with the exception of money and finance (Figure 2.5).

Figure 2.3: Comparison of the Old and the New Global Integration Indexes

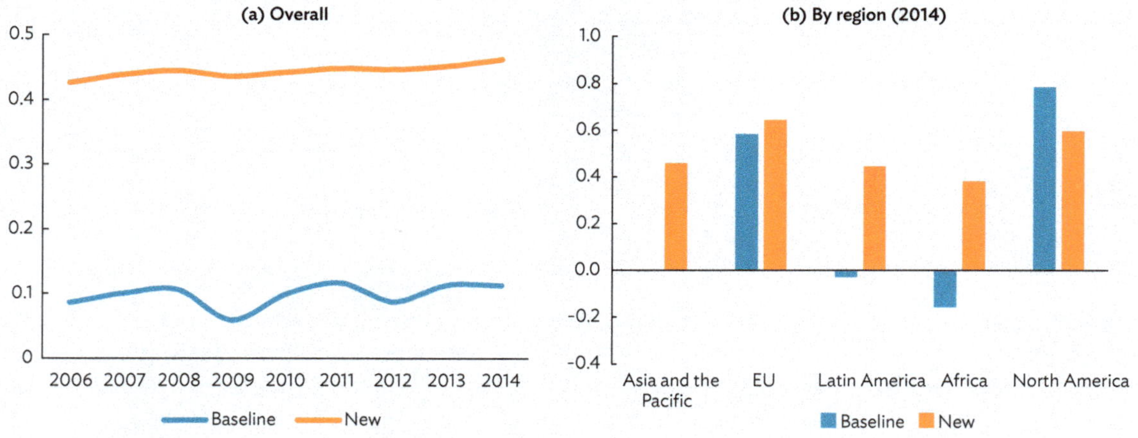

(a) Overall
0.5
0.4
0.3
0.2
0.1
0
2006 2007 2008 2009 2010 2011 2012 2013 2014
Baseline
New
(b) By region (2014)
1.0
0.8
0.6
0.4
0.2
0.0
-0.2
-0.4
Asia and the Pacific
EU
Latin America
Africa
North America
Baseline
New

EU = European Union.

Sources: Asian Development Bank calculations using data from Huh, H. S. and C. Y. Park. 2021. A New Index of Globalization: Measuring Impacts of Integration on Economic Growth and Income Inequality. *The World Economy*. 44 (2). pp. 409–43; ADB. Asia-Pacific Regional Cooperation and Integration Index Database. https://aric.adb.org/database/arcii (accessed November 2023).

Figure 2.4: Comparison of Dimensional Indexes, 2014

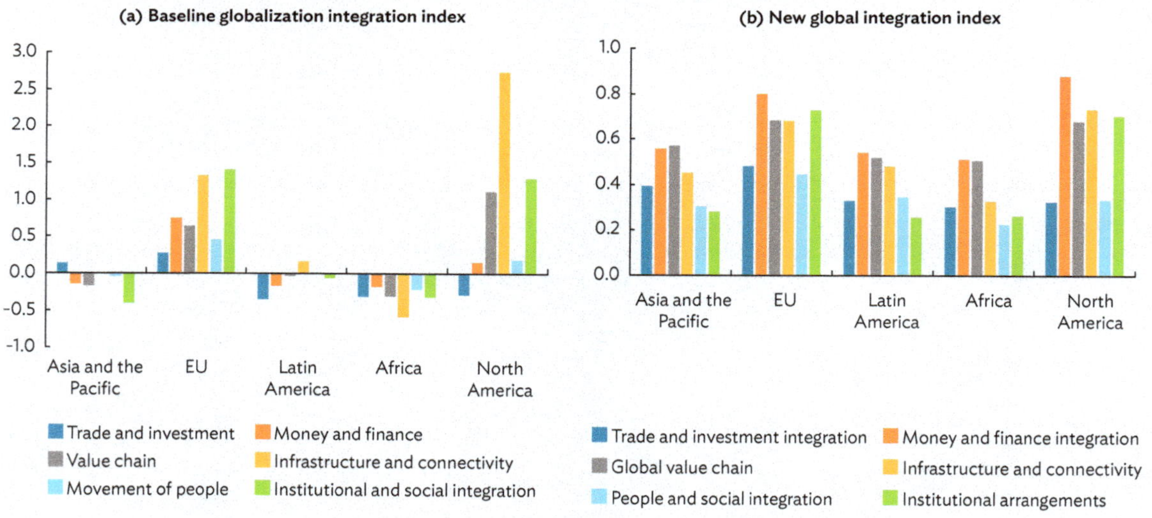

(a) Baseline globalization integration index
3.0
2.5
2.0
1.5
1.0
0.5
0.0
-0.5
-1.0
Asia and the Pacific
EU
Latin America
Africa
North America
Trade and investment
Money and finance
Value chain
Infrastructure and connectivity
Movement of people
Institutional and social integration
(b) New global integration index
1.0
0.8
0.6
0.4
0.2
0.0
Asia and the Pacific
EU
Latin America
Africa
North America
Trade and investment integration
Money and finance integration
Global value chain
Infrastructure and connectivity
People and social integration
Institutional arrangements

EU = European Union.

Sources: Asian Development Bank calculations using data from Huh, H. and C. Y. Park. 2021. A New Index of Globalization: Measuring Impacts of Integration on Economic Growth and Income Inequality. *The World Economy*. 44 (2). pp. 409–43; ADB. Asia-Pacific Regional Cooperation and Integration Index Database. https://aric.adb.org/database/arcii (accessed November 2023).

Figure 2.5: Correlations between the Baseline and New Global Integration Index, 2014

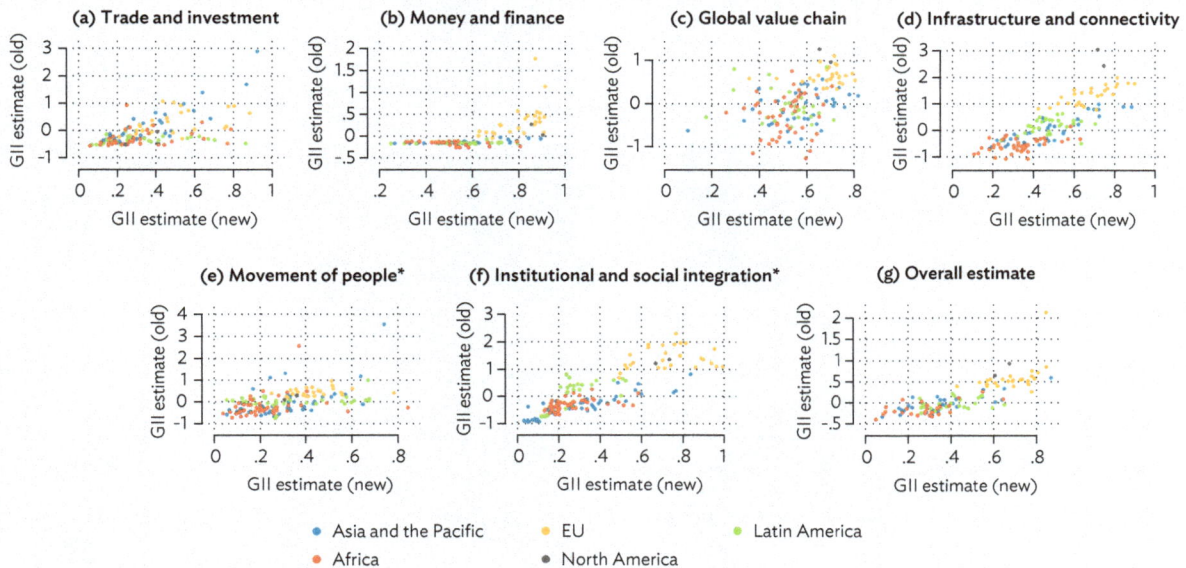

EU = European Union

Sources: Asian Development Bank calculations using data from Huh, H. and C. Y. Park. 2021. A New Index of Globalization: Measuring Impacts of Integration on Economic Growth and Income Inequality. *The World Economy.* 44 (2). pp. 409–43; ADB. Asia-Pacific Regional Cooperation and Integration Index Database. https://aric.adb.org/database/arcii (accessed November 2023).

2.4 Trends in Global Integration

Global interconnectedness has increased in the past 2 decades, propelled by fast-paced developments in technology and greater mobility in goods, services, capital, and labor. Deepening of interdependencies has reshaped cross-border channels of cooperation, with some economies embedding global integration efforts in their industrial and economic policies. For example, EU economies have sealed free trade agreements with Asian economies such as Japan, the Republic of Korea, and Singapore—and with the Association of Southeast Asian Nations (ASEAN), the most dynamic economic bloc in the region (Khanna 2021). Such integration efforts have led global flows of goods, capital, and technology increase (Figure 2.6).

Asia's Growing Importance in Global Linkages

Alongside the rise in global integration, Asia's importance in the global economy has increased. Between 2006 and 2021, Asia's goods trade increased substantially. In 2021, the region accounted for over one-third of global trade in goods. The large proportion of patents filed by economies in Asia and the Pacific (over 50% of the global total) reflects vibrant innovation-related activities in the region. This may also be marked by Asia's heavy investment on technology-based startups and research and development (Tonby et al. 2019). Finally, while Asia generates more than 50% of global annual CO_2 emissions, the region's significant share of environmental goods trade may reflect growing efforts to target environmentally friendly products for trade, to curb pollutive industries, and address concerns over climate change.

Figure 2.6: Trends in Global Flows

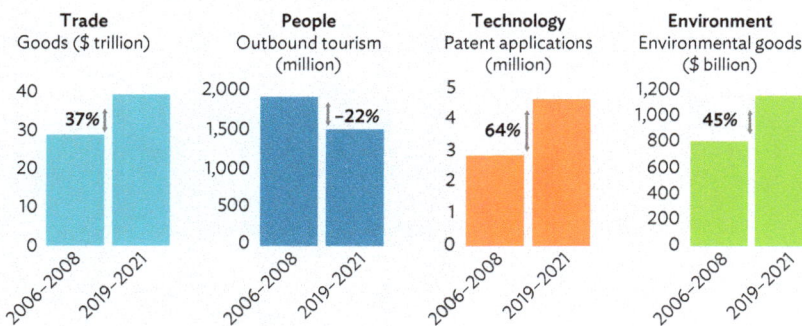

Trends in global flows

Trade Goods ($ trillion)	People Outbound tourism (million)	Technology Patent applications (million)	Environment Environmental goods ($ billion)
37%	−22%	64%	45%

Asia's share in global flows, 2021 (% of total)

38	4	56	45

Sources: ADB calculations using data from World Intellectual Property Organization (WIPO). WIPO IP Statistics Data Center. https://www3.wipo.int/ipstats/ (accessed May 2023); International Monetary Fund (IMF). Direction of Trade Statistics. https://www.imf.org/en/Data (accessed July 2023); United Nations. Commodity Trade Database. https://comtrade.un.org (accessed May 2023); United Nations World Tourism Organization. Tourism Satellite Accounts. http://statistics.unwto.org (accessed May 2023).

The upward trend of the GII suggests that global integration has generally increased (Figure 2.7).[3] In general, most economies having GII estimates in 2006 and 2021 became more globalized over this period, with some exceptions (Annex 3a). Despite the overall improvement, some downturns in global integration are also noticeable. These include during the 2008–2009 global financial crisis and the 2011–2012 euro area debt crisis. A third downturn in 2015 and 2016 can be attributed to the global stock market rout, stoked by concerns over the PRC's slowing economy, the Fed's interest rate increase, Brexit, and wild swings in oil prices. More recently, a slight retreat in global integration took place in 2020 during the COVID-19 pandemic.

Consistently across years, the Netherlands is shown to be the most globalized economy. Other EU economies also reported high estimates (Annex 3a). Mexico achieved the highest global integration estimate in Latin America, followed closely by the Bahamas. For the Middle East, the United Arab Emirates, and Bahrain are the most globalized. Meanwhile, estimates for African economies tend to be at the lower end of the spectrum, with the notable exceptions of Mauritius, Morocco, and South Africa.

---

[3]   Comparison of the GII and the KOF globalization index show high correlation. It would be interesting to compare the GII with other composite globalization indexes. To the best of knowledge, only the KOF globalization index (Dreher, Gaston, and Martens 2008; Gygli et al. 2018) has been updated to include recent years (https://www.kof.ethz.ch/). The correlation between the GII and KOF globalization index was 0.89 from 2006 to 2018. The range of the correlation over this period was 0.87 to 0.91.

Figure 2.7: Global Integration Index (average, maximum, and minimum)

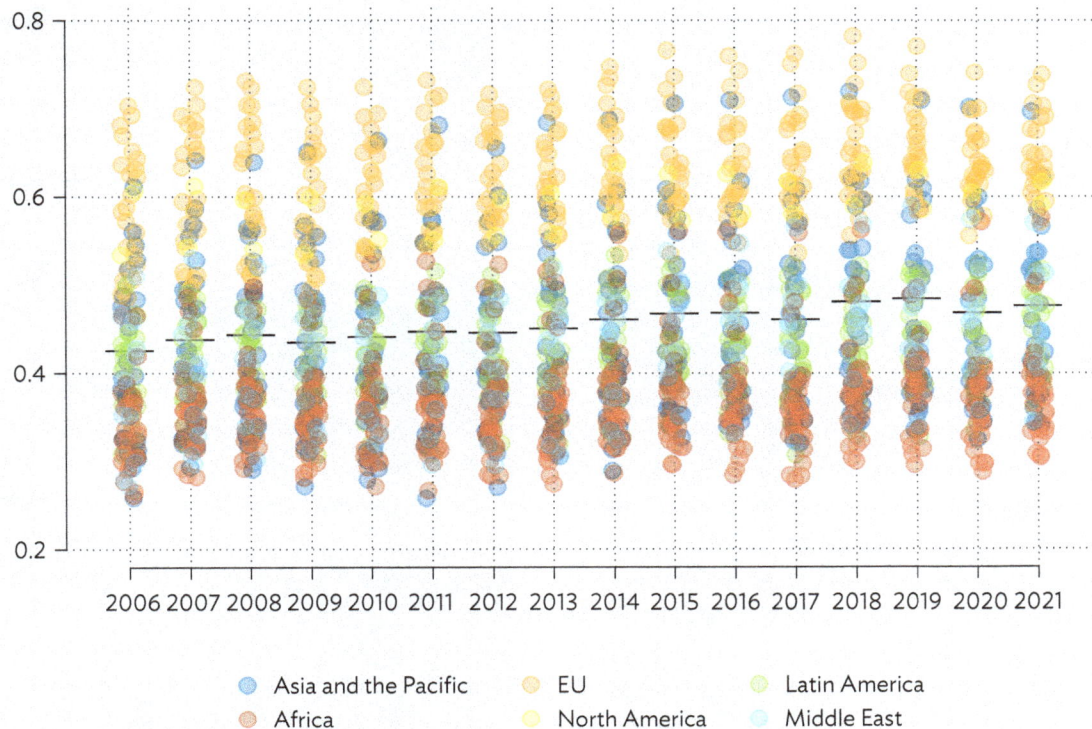

Asia and the Pacific   EU   Latin America

Africa   North America   Middle East

EU = European Union.

Notes: The gray line represents the average globalization index for all economies included in the sample for each year. Meanwhile, the circles represent the global integration index for each economy.

Source: Asian Development Bank. Asia-Pacific Regional Cooperation and Integration Index Database. https://aric.adb.org/database/arcii (accessed November 2023).

Among economies in Asia and the Pacific, Singapore registered the highest global integration estimate in 2021, comparable to EU economies such as Belgium and the United Kingdom. Singapore's high level of globalization can be attributed to its strategies aimed at reinforcing economic openness to overcome its limited resources. As a small economy, engaging with global markets was a necessity for Singapore during its early years (Lai-to 2000). Singapore offered a low-cost base for multinational corporations to conduct labor-intensive operations, which effectively reduced unemployment by the early 1970s. Over time, Singapore's openness to trade and investment has allowed it to continuously raise its productive and technological capabilities, leading to its evolution into a high-value-added manufacturing hub in the 1990s and 2000s (Lai-to 2000). Multinationals have not only boosted their presence in Singapore but have also expanded their operations to include research and development (R&D), logistics and distribution, fund management, and technical support. The strong reliance of Singapore on the free movement of capital also makes it a crucial hub and financial center for Southeast Asia (Robinson 2019).

Results by Region and Income Group

By income group, high-income economies are the best performers in global integration, and the gap with other income groups is substantial (Figure 2.8a).[4] The upper-middle and lower-middle income groups follow, while low-income economies tend to be least globally integrated. These rankings affirm the strong association between global economic integration and economic development. Between 2006 and 2021, average growth in the global integration index ranged from 10% to 14%, with upper-middle-income economies showing most progress. The performance of high-income and upper-middle economies was wider-ranging than among low or low-middle economies, whose performance is consistently low (Figure 2.8b).

Figure 2.8: Global Integration Index by Income Level

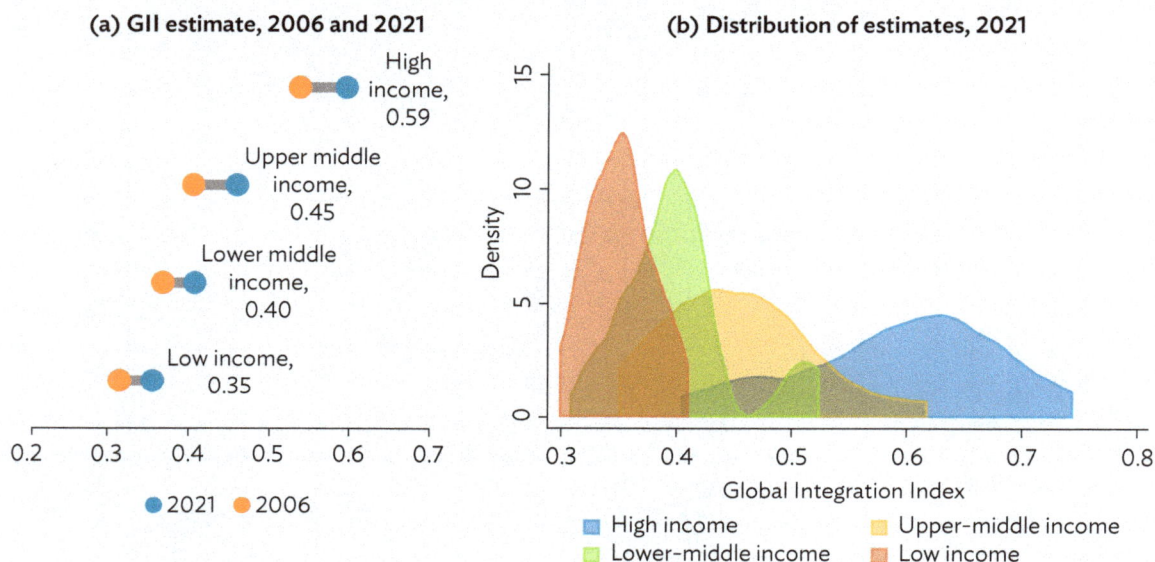

(a) GII estimate, 2006 and 2021

(b) Distribution of estimates, 2021

● 2021 ● 2006

GII = Global Integration Index.

Sources: Asian Development Bank calculations using data from ADB. Asia-Pacific Regional Cooperation and Integration Index Database. https://aric.adb.org/database/arcii; World Bank. World Development Indicators. https://databank.worldbank.org/source/world-developmentindicators (all accessed November 2023).

Performance by income group across dimensions shows a similar picture, except for environmental cooperation. Except for the environmental dimension, high-income economies are more globally integrated than other income groups (Figure 2.9). The lower-middle and low-income groups have the lowest estimates. After 2019, all income groups experienced a significant slowdown in trade and investment and people and social integration, confirming the disrupting effect of the pandemic. In the case of environmental cooperation, low and lower-middle income economies report the highest performance, followed by upper-middle and high income economies. Notably, higher income economies report low estimates in this dimension: Examples include six oil exporters in the Middle East, high-income economies such as Belgium, Luxembourg, Singapore, and the United States, and

---

[4]   The income groupings are based on the World Bank income classification (e.g., Fantom and Serajuddin 2016), which comprises four groups: high income (with 53 economies in our sample of 173 economies), upper-middle income (45), lower-middle income (53), and low income (22).

upper-middle income economies, including Angola, Iran, and Türkiye. These have high carbon emissions and deep ecological footprints—both inversely related to environmental cooperation. Such findings tend to reinforce that deleterious effects on the environment can increase with income. Between income groups, however, differences in performance in environmental cooperation are small.

Figure 2.9: Dimensions of the Global Integration Index, by Income Level

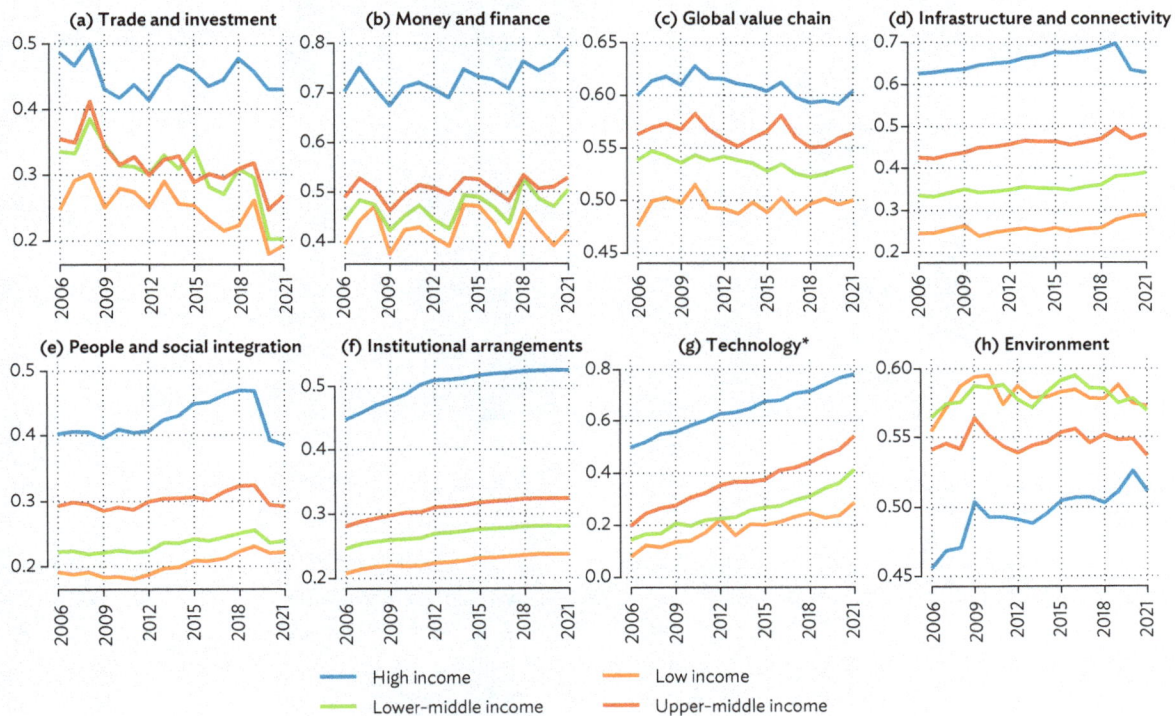

Technology* = Technology and Digital Connectivity.

Sources: Asian Development Bank calculations using data from ADB. Asia-Pacific Regional Cooperation and Integration Index Database. https://aric.adb.org/database/arcii; World Bank. World Development Indicators. https://databank.worldbank.org/source/world-developmentindicators (all accessed November 2023).

By region, the EU presents the highest level of global integration, followed by North America (Figure 2.10a). This is consistent with the trend observed in Figure 2.8 since most economies in the EU and North America belong to the high-income group, except for Bulgaria and Romania which are upper-middle income economies. Asia and the Pacific follows the EU and North America, and the Middle East and Latin America are next. Regional estimates also suggest Africa is the least globalized region. Developing regions are catching up with the EU and North America even as the gap in global integration levels remains. Asia and the Pacific, for example, exhibited 14% growth in average global integration. North America showed the lowest growth progress, at about 4%.

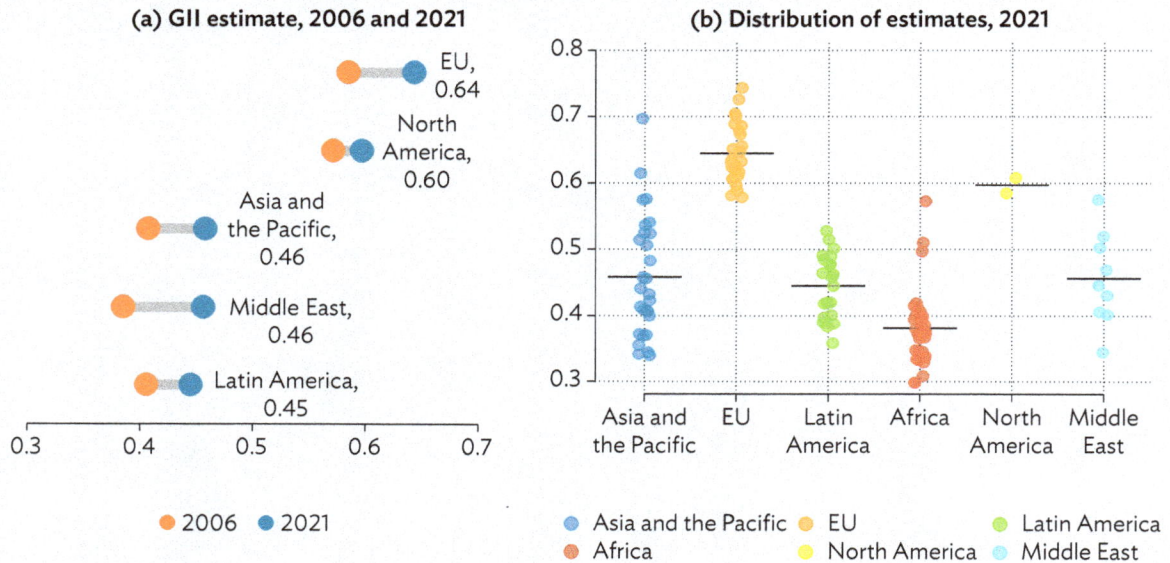

Figure 2.10: Global Integration Index, by Region

(a) GII estimate, 2006 and 2021

EU, 0.64

North America, 0.60

Asia and the Pacific, 0.46

Middle East, 0.46

Latin America, 0.45

● 2006   ● 2021

(b) Distribution of estimates, 2021

Asia and the Pacific | EU | Latin America
Africa | North America | Middle East

EU = European Union, GII = Global Integration Index.

Source: Asian Development Bank. Asia-Pacific Regional Cooperation and Integration Index Database. https://aric.adb.org/database/arcii (accessed November 2023).

Across dimensions, the EU is the most globally integrated region, followed by North America and Asia and the Pacific (Figure 2.11). Trends by dimension are largely consistent with overall global integration estimates by region. For trade and investment, Asia and the Pacific performs below the EU but above the Middle East, Africa, and Latin America. The impact of COVID-19 is also noticeable in some dimensional indexes by region, particularly in trade and investment and people and social integration. In both dimensions and across all regions, the decline was significant and regions have yet to reach their pre-pandemic levels of global integration. For environmental cooperation, regional performance is broadly similar across regions, with the Middle East the outlier. However, this region tends to perform better than other developing regions in other dimensions, particularly in infrastructure and connectivity, institutional arrangements, and technology and digital connectivity.

East Asia and Southeast Asia take the lead in global integration among the subregions. East Asia stands out across multiple dimensions, including money and finance, infrastructure and connectivity, people and social integration, institutional arrangements, and technology and digital connectivity. In contrast, Southeast Asia has seen strong growth in trade and investment integration, and is also deeply involved in global value chains (Figure 2.12). These subregions have been considered the "factory of the world" for more than 2 decades, accounting for 18.4% of global inward foreign direct investment in 2019 (Shepherd and Prakash 2021). The rise of East Asia and Southeast Asia in global manufacturing can be attributed to a combination of factors such as natural resource endowments, advantageous starting conditions, government policies, and the strategic decisions of individual companies (Kawai and Wignaraja 2014). Additionally, these subregions appear to be at the forefront of the digital revolution. For instance, the top economies with the largest share of patents include the PRC; the Republic of Korea; Malaysia; and Taipei,China. Japan and Singapore also outperform the US and the Organisation for Economic Co-operation and Development (Sedik et al. 2019). In contrast, South Asia and Central Asia tend to lag in terms of global integration comparatively.

Figure 2.11: Dimensions of the Global Integration Index, by Region

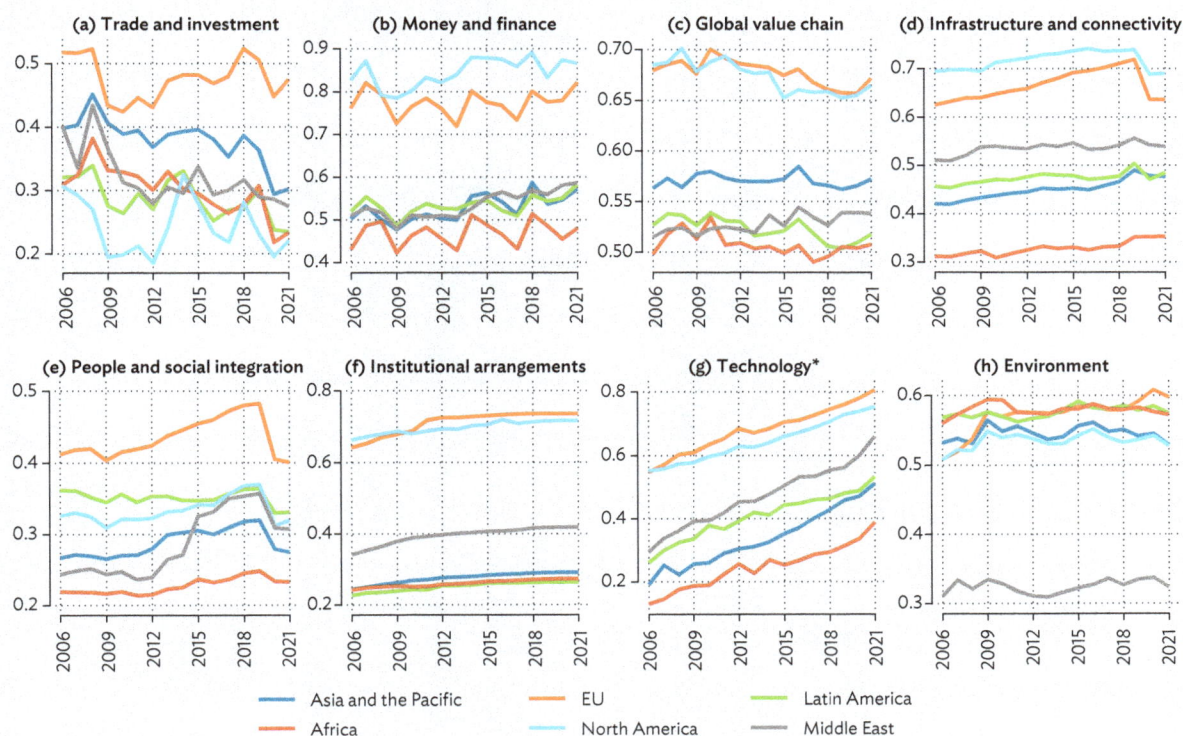

Technology* = technology and digital connectivity, EU = European Union.

Source: Asian Development Bank. Asia-Pacific Regional Cooperation and Integration Index Database. https://aric.adb.org/database/arcii (accessed November 2023).

The GII can also inform progress in global integration of Asian subregional initiatives with the rest of the world (Figure 2.13). When considering estimates by subregional initiative, the Indonesia-Malaysia-Thailand Growth Triangle (IMT-GT) counts as the most globally integrated initiative from 2006 to 2021. These results might be driven by high global integration of member economies outside the subregional initiative. Other initiatives showing strong global integration are the Brunei Darussalam–Indonesia–Malaysia–Philippines East ASEAN Growth Area (BIMP-EAGA), ASEAN, and Greater Mekong Subregion (GMS), all composed mainly of Southeast Asian economies. The South Asian Association for Regional Cooperation (SAARC) and South Asia Subregional Economic Cooperation (SASEC) obtained the lowest estimates in the overall index. Most subregional initiatives show increases in global integration from 2006 to 2021, with the Bay of Bengal Initiative for Multi-Sectoral Technical and Economic Cooperation (BIMSTEC) having the highest growth rate during the period.

Figure 2.12: Dimensions of the Global Integration Index, by Asian Subregion

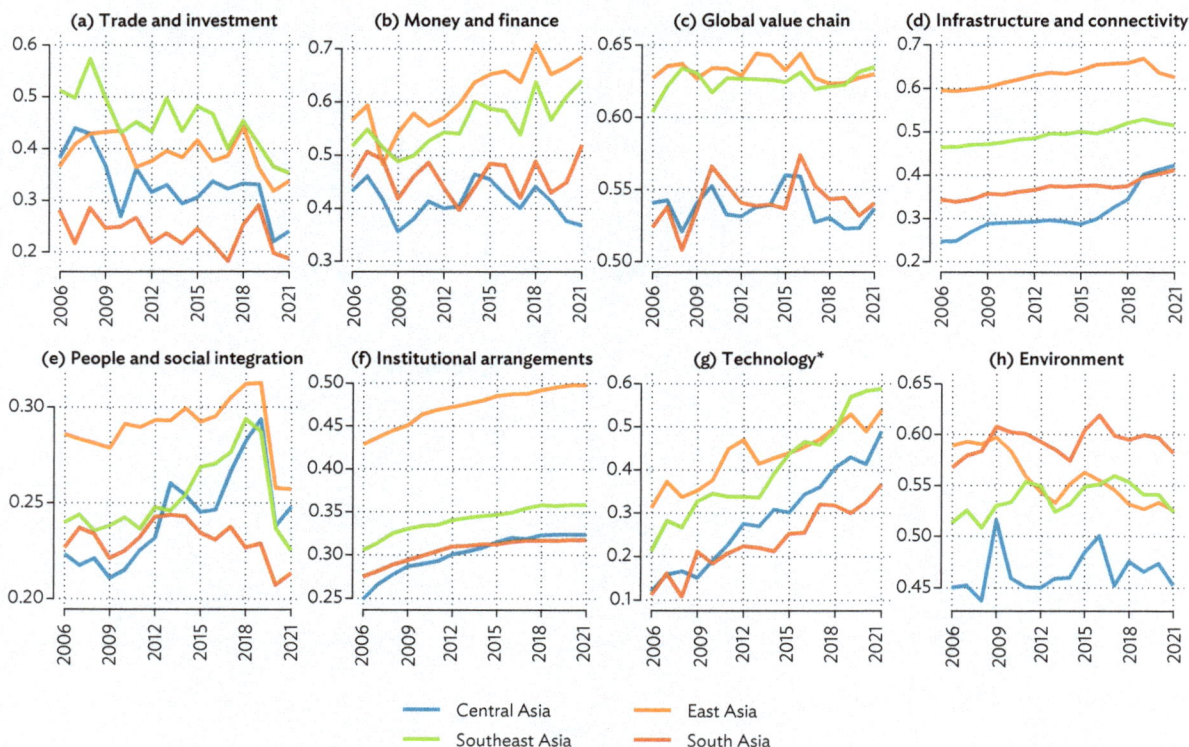

Technology* = technology and digital connectivity.

Source: Asian Development Bank. Asia-Pacific Regional Cooperation and Integration Index Database. https://aric.adb.org/database/arcii (accessed November 2023).

Overall trends in the GII underscore different trajectories of globalization. While most economies have witnessed increasing levels of global integration, the pace and trajectory across dimensions suggest a more wide-ranging picture across regions and income levels. Flows in trade and investment, people and social integration, and infrastructure and connectivity were generally steady for Asia and the Pacific but contracted in recent years. Other dimensions, including institutional arrangements and technology and digital connectivity, suggest more stable, or even increasing, levels of global integration. These differences need to be considered when assessing impacts of global integration on development outcomes, which is the subject of inquiry in Chapter 4.

Figure 2.13: Global Integration Index, by Subregional Initiative

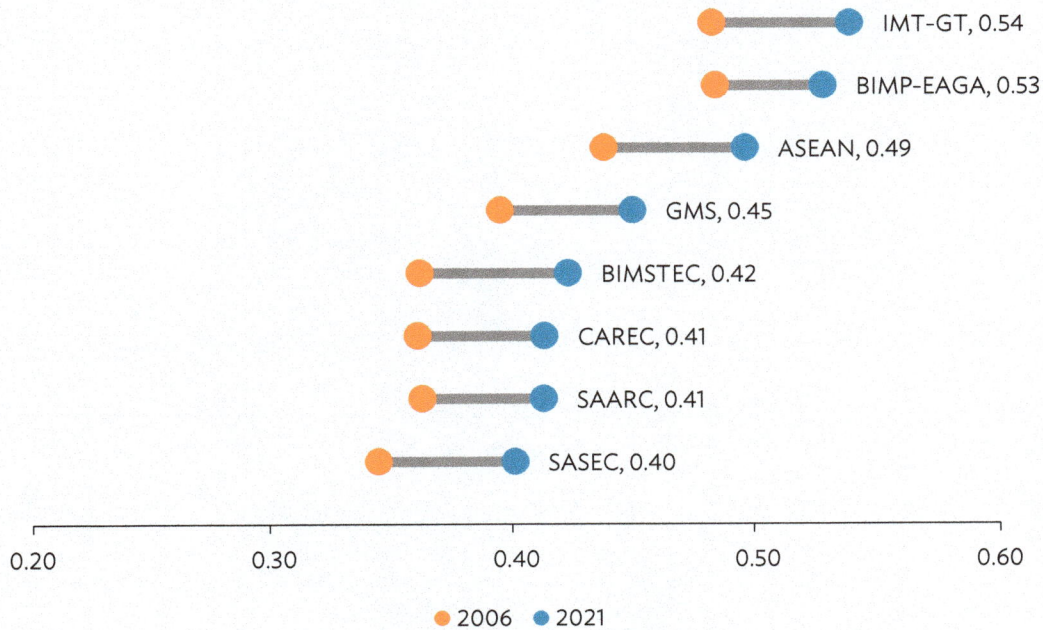

IMT-GT, 0.54

BIMP-EAGA, 0.53

ASEAN, 0.49

GMS, 0.45

BIMSTEC, 0.42

CAREC, 0.41

SAARC, 0.41

SASEC, 0.40

| 0.20 | 0.30 | 0.40 | 0.50 | 0.60 |

● 2006   ● 2021

ASEAN = Association of Southeast Asian Nations, BIMP-EAGA = Brunei Darussalam–Indonesia–Malaysia–Philippines East ASEAN Growth Area, BIMSTEC = Bay of Bengal Initiative for Multi-Sectoral Technical and Economic Cooperation, CAREC = Central Asia Regional Economic Cooperation, GMS = Greater Mekong Subregion, IMT-GT = Indonesia–Malaysia–Thailand Growth Triangle, SAARC = South Asian Association for Regional Cooperation, SASEC = South Asia Subregional Economic Cooperation.

Source: Asian Development Bank. Asia-Pacific Regional Cooperation and Integration Index Database. https://aric.adb.org/database/arcii (accessed November 2023).

References

Altman, S. and C. Bastian. 2023. *DHL Global Interconnectedness Index 2022: An In-depth Report on the State of Globalization.* San Francisco, CA: DHL.

Asian Development Bank (ADB). 2020. *Asian Development Outlook (ADO) 2020: What Drives Innovation in Asia?* Manila.

———. 2021a. *Asia-Pacific Regional Cooperation and Integration Index: Enhanced Framework, Analysis and Applications.* Manila.

———. 2021b. *Asian Economic Integration Report 2021: Making Digital Platform Works for Asia and the Pacific.* Manila.

———. 2021c. *Asia-Pacific Trade Facilitation Report 2021: Supply Chains of Critical Goods Amid the COVID-19 Pandemic—Disruptions, Recovery, and Resilience.* Manila.

———. 2022. *Asian Economic Integration Report 2022: Advancing Digital Services Trade in Asia and the Pacific.* Manila.

Chinn, M. D. and H. Ito. 2006. What Matters for Financial Development? Capital Controls, Institutions, and Interactions. *Journal of Development Economics.* 81(1). pp. 163-192.

Dreher, A., N. Gaston, and P. Martens. 2008. *Measuring Globalisation: Gauging Its Consequences.* New York: Springer Science and Business Media.

Dür, A., L. Baccini, and M. Elsig. 2014. The Design of International Trade Agreements: Introducing a New Database. *The Review of International Organizations.* 9(3). pp. 353-375.

Fantom, N. and U. Serajuddin. 2016. The World Bank's Classification of Countries by Income. *Policy Research Working Paper.* No. 7528. Washington, DC: World Bank.

Figge, L. and P. Martens. 2014. Globalisation Continues: The Maastricht Globalisation Index Revisited and Updated. *Globalizations.* 11. pp. 875–893.

Friedlingstein, P., M. O'Sullivan, M. W. Jones, R. M. Andrew, L. Gregor, J. Hauck, C. Le Quéré et al. 2022. Global Carbon Budget 2022. *Earth System Science Data.* 14 (11).pp. 4811–4900.

Gygli, S., F. Haelg, and J-E. Sturm. 2018. The KOF Globalization Index - Revisited. *KOF Working Paper.* No. 439. KOF Swiss Economic Institute.

Gwartney, J. and R. Lawson. 2001. *Economic Freedom of the World: 2001 Annual Report.* Vancouver: Fraser Institute.

Huh, H. S. and C. Y. Park. 2021. A New Index of Globalization: Measuring Impacts of Integration on Economic Growth and Income Inequality. *The World Economy.* 44 (2). pp. 409–443.

Kawai, M. and G. Wignaraja. 2014. Trade Policy and Growth in Asia. *ADBI Working Paper Series.* No. 495. Tokyo: Asian Development Bank Institute.

Khanna, P. 2021. The Next Wave of Globalization: Asia in the Cockpit. *Nikkei Asia*. 13 January. https://asia.nikkei. com/Spotlight/The-Big-Story/The-next-wave-of-globalization-Asia-in-the-cockpit.

Lai-to, L. 2000. Singapore's Globalization Strategy. *East Asia: An International Quarterly*. 18 (2). pp. 36–49.

Molinuevo, M. and S. Sáez. 2014. *Regulatory Assessment Toolkit: A Practical Methodology for Assessing Regulation on Trade and Investment in Services*. Trade and Development. Washington, DC: World Bank. http://hdl.handle. net/10986/17255.

Organisation for Economic Co-operation and Development (OECD). 2008. *Handbook on Constructing Composite Indicators: Methodology and User Guide*. Paris: OECD Publishing.

Park, C. Y. and R. Claveria. 2018. Constructing the Asia-Pacific Regional Cooperation and Integration Index: A Panel Approach. *ADB Economics Working Papers Series*. No. 544. Manila: ADB.

Robinson, E. 2019. *Globalisation in a Small Open Economy: The Singapore Experience*. Basel: Bank for International Settlements.

Sedik, T. S., S. Chen, T. Feyzioglu, M. Ghazanchyan, S. Gupta, S. Jahan, J. M. Jauregui, et al. 2019. The Digital Revolution in Asia and Its Macroeconomic Effects. *ADBI Working Paper Series*. No. 1029. Tokyo: Asian Development Bank Institute.

Shepherd, B. and A. Prakash. 2021. *Global Value Chains and Investment: Changing Dynamics in Asia*. Jakarta: Economic Research Institute for ASEAN and East Asia.

Tonby, O., J. Woetzel, W. Choi, K. Eloot, R. Dhawan, J. Seong, and P. Wang. 2019. *The Future of Asia: Asian Flows and Networks are Defining the Next Phase of Globalization*. McKinsey Global Institute. https://www.mckinsey.com/ featured-insights/asia-pacific/the-future-of-asia-asian-flows-and-networks-are-defining-the-next-phase-of-globalization.

United Nations Conference on Trade and Development. 2022. Total Trade in Services. *Fact Sheet 5*. https://unctad. org/system/files/official-document/tdstat47_FS05_en.pdf.

World Trade Organization (WTO). 2019. *World Trade Report 2019: The Future of Services Trade*. Geneva.

———. 2022. *World Trade Report 2022: Climate Change and International Trade*. Geneva.

Annex 2.1: Economies in the Global Integration Index and Regional Integration Index

Region	Economies
Asia and the Pacific (48)	Armenia; Australia; Azerbaijan; Bangladesh; Bhutan; Brunei Darussalam; Cambodia; Cook Islands; Federated States of Micronesia; Fiji; Georgia; Hong Kong, China; India; Indonesia; Japan; Kazakhstan; Kiribati; Kyrgyz Republic; Lao People's Democratic Republic; Malaysia; Maldives; Marshall Islands; Mongolia; Nauru; Nepal; New Zealand; Pakistan; Palau; Papua New Guinea; Philippines; People's Republic of China; Republic of Korea; Samoa; Singapore; Solomon Islands; Sri Lanka; Taipei,China; Tajikistan; Thailand; Timor-Leste; Tonga; Turkmenistan; Tuvalu; Uzbekistan; Vanuatu; Viet Nam
EU (27)	Austria, Belgium, Bulgaria, Cyprus, Czech Republic, Denmark, Estonia, Finland, France, Germany, Greece, Hungary, Ireland, Italy, Latvia, Lithuania, Luxembourg, Malta, Netherlands, Poland, Portugal, Romania, Slovak Republic, Slovenia, Spain, Sweden, United Kingdom
Latin America (32)	Antigua & Barbuda, Argentina, Bahamas, Barbados, Belize, Bolivia, Brazil, Chile, Colombia, Costa Rica, Dominica, Dominican Republic, Ecuador, El Salvador, Grenada, Guatemala, Guyana, Haiti, Honduras, Jamaica, Mexico, Nicaragua, Panama, Paraguay, Peru, St. Kitts & Nevis, St. Lucia, St. Vincent & the Grenadines, Suriname, Trinidad & Tobago, Uruguay, Venezuela
Africa (49)	Algeria, Angola, Benin, Botswana, Burkina Faso, Burundi, Cameroon, Cape Verde, Central African Republic, Chad, Comoros, Congo Democratic Republic, Congo Republic, Cote d'Ivoire, Djibouti, Equatorial Guinea, Eritrea, Ethiopia, Gabon, Gambia, Ghana, Guinea, Guinea-Bissau, Kenya, Lesotho, Liberia, Madagascar, Malawi, Mali, Mauritius, Morocco, Mozambique, Namibia, Niger, Nigeria, Rwanda, Sao Tome & Principe, Senegal, Seychelles, Sierra Leone, South Africa, Sudan, Swaziland (Eswatini), Tanzania, Togo, Tunisia, Uganda, Zambia, Zimbabwe
Middle East (15)	Bahrain, Iran, Iraq, Israel, Jordan, Kuwait, Lebanon, Oman, Qatar, Saudi Arabia, Syria, Türkiye, United Arab Emirates, West Bank and Gaza, Yemen
North America (2)	Canada, United States

Source: Asian Development Bank.

Annex 2.2: Principal Component Analysis and Weights for Aggregation

Table 2.2.1: Global Integration Index

Number of principal components and implied weights: Dimensions

Dimension P1

Number	1	2	3	4	5	6
Eigenvalue	2.93	1.27	1.01	0.40	0.25	0.13
Cum Prop	0.49	0.70	0.87	0.94	0.98	1.00
Indicator	P1a	P1b	P1c	P1d	P1e	P1f
Weight	0.17	0.15	0.17	0.15	0.18	0.18

Dimension P2

Number	1	2	3	4	5
Eigenvalue	2.22	0.98	0.92	0.64	0.27
Cum Prop	0.44	0.64	0.82	0.95	1.00
Indicator	P2a	P2b	P2c	P2d	P2e
Weight	0.18	0.20	0.24	0.14	0.23

Dimension P3

Number	1	2	3	4	5
Eigenvalue	2.22	1.10	0.83	0.47	0.38
Cum Prop	0.44	0.66	0.83	0.92	1.00
Indicator	P3a	P3b	P3c	P3d	P3e
Weight	0.18	0.18	0.22	0.21	0.20

Dimension P4

Number	1	2	3	4	5
Eigenvalue	3.08	0.83	0.59	0.37	0.13
Cum Prop	0.62	0.78	0.90	0.97	1.00
Indicator	P4a	P4b	P4c	P4d	P4e
Weight	0.19	0.20	0.18	0.22	0.21

Dimension P5

Number	1	2	3	4	5	6
Eigenvalue	2.20	1.37	0.97	0.64	0.50	0.33
Cum Prop	0.37	0.59	0.75	0.86	0.95	1.00
Indicator	P5a	P5b	P5c	P5d	P5e	P5f
Weight	0.15	0.16	0.17	0.21	0.13	0.18

Dimension P6

Number	1	2	3	4	5	6
Eigenvalue	3.64	0.80	0.25	0.20	0.12	
Cum Prop	0.73	0.89	0.94	0.98	1.00	
Indicator	P6a	P6b	P6c	P6d	P6e	P6f
Weight	0.11	0.23	0.24	0.22	0.20	0.17

Dimension P7

Number	1	2	3	4	5	6
Eigenvalue	3.17	0.97	0.74	0.53	0.43	0.15
Cum Prop	0.53	0.69	0.81	0.90	0.98	1.00
Indicator	P7a	P7b	P7c	P7d	P7e	P7f
Weight	0.13	0.16	0.21	0.21	0.15	0.15

Dimension P8

Number	1	2	3	4	5
Eigenvalue	2.02	0.98	0.61	0.39	
Cum Prop	0.51	0.75	0.90	1.00	
Indicator	P8a	P8b	P8c	P8d	P8e
Weight	0.21	0.26	0.24	0.29	

Number of principal components and implied weights: Overall

Number	1	2	3	4	5	6	7	8
Eigenvalue	3.93	1.66	0.84	0.51	0.39	0.27	0.23	0.17
Cum Prop	0.49	0.70	0.80	0.87	0.92	0.95	0.98	1.00
Dimension	1	2	3	4	5	6	7	8
Weight	0.11	0.12	0.11	0.13	0.12	0.13	0.12	0.15

Note: The "Cum Prop" row reports the cumulated proportion of total variation in the data accounted for by the principal components. The values highlighted in red are the principal components chosen for the aggregation.

Source: Asian Development Bank. Asia-Pacific Regional Cooperation and Integration Index Database. https://aric.adb.org/database/arcii (accessed November 2023).

Table 2.2.2: Regional Integration Index

Number of principal components and implied weights: Dimensions

Asia and the Pacific

Dimension P1

Number	1	2	3	4
Eigenvalue	2.59	0.86	0.45	0.10
Cum Prop	0.65	0.86	0.98	1.00

Indicator	P1a	P1b	P1e	P1f
Weight	0.24	0.21	0.28	0.27

Dimension P2

Number	1	2	3	4	5
Eigenvalue	2.10	1.22	0.82	0.64	0.22
Cum Prop	0.42	0.67	0.83	0.96	1.00

Indicator	P2a	P2b	P2c	P2d	P2e
Weight	0.20	0.20	0.21	0.16	0.23

Dimension P3

Number	1	2	3	4	5
Eigenvalue	1.80	1.21	0.88	0.68	0.43
Cum Prop	0.36	0.60	0.78	0.91	1.00

Indicator	P3a	P3b	P3c	P3d	P3e
Weight	0.23	0.20	0.21	0.21	0.15

Dimension P4

Number	1	2	3	4	5
Eigenvalue	3.02	0.99	0.60	0.26	0.14
Cum Prop	0.60	0.80	0.92	0.97	1.00

Indicator	P4a	P4b	P4c	P4d	P4e
Weight	0.21	0.20	0.19	0.21	0.19

Dimension P5

Number	1	2	3	4	5	6
Eigenvalue	2.10	1.26	0.80	0.76	0.57	0.51
Cum Prop	0.35	0.56	0.69	0.82	0.92	1.00

Indicator	P5a	P5b	P5c	P5d	P5e	P5f
Weight	0.18	0.12	0.18	0.15	0.21	0.16

Dimension P6

Number	1	2	3	4	5
Eigenvalue	3.81	0.51	0.29	0.22	0.16
Cum Prop	0.76	0.87	0.92	0.97	1.00

Indicator	P6a	P6b	P6c	P6d	P6e
Weight	0.16	0.21	0.22	0.20	0.22

Dimension P7

Number	1	2	3	4	5	6
Eigenvalue	3.06	1.06	0.71	0.61	0.39	0.17
Cum Prop	0.51	0.69	0.80	0.91	0.97	1.00

Indicator	P7a	P7b	P7c	P7d	P7e	P7f
Weight	0.16	0.16	0.17	0.20	0.15	0.15

Dimension P8

Number	1	2	3	4
Eigenvalue	1.84	1.11	0.78	0.26
Cum Prop	0.46	0.74	0.93	1.00

Indicator	P8a	P8b	P8c	P8d
Weight	0.25	0.28	0.16	0.31

Number of principal components and implied weights: Overall

Number	1	2	3	4	5	6	7	8
Eigenvalue	3.32	2.12	0.89	0.67	0.38	0.29	0.21	0.13
Cum Prop	0.41	0.68	0.79	0.87	0.92	0.96	0.98	1.00

Indicator	P1	P2	P3	P4	P5	P6	P7	P8
Weight	0.13	0.13	0.13	0.14	0.12	0.13	0.14	0.11

Number of principal components and implied weights: Dimensions

EU

Dimension P1

Number	1	2	3	4
Eigenvalue	1.99	1.61	0.21	0.19
Cum Prop	0.50	0.90	0.95	1.00

Indicator	P1a	P1b	P1e	P1f
Weight	0.25	0.25	0.25	0.25

Dimension P2

Number	1	2	3	4	5
Eigenvalue	1.46	1.25	1.09	0.69	0.51
Cum Prop	0.29	0.54	0.76	0.90	1.00

Indicator	P2a	P2b	P2c	P2d	P2e
Weight	0.20	0.20	0.18	0.20	0.22

Dimension P3

Number	1	2	3	4	5
Eigenvalue	2.06	1.09	0.95	0.57	0.32
Cum Prop	0.41	0.63	0.82	0.94	1.00

Indicator	P3a	P3b	P3c	P3d	P3e
Weight	0.19	0.19	0.20	0.19	0.23

Dimension P4

Number	1	2	3	4	5
Eigenvalue	2.23	1.31	0.84	0.34	0.28
Cum Prop	0.45	0.71	0.88	0.94	1.00

Indicator	P4a	P4b	P4c	P4d	P4e
Weight	0.20	0.23	0.21	0.19	0.18

Dimension P5

Number	1	2	3	4	5	6
Eigenvalue	1.89	1.40	0.99	0.77	0.67	0.28
Cum Prop	0.31	0.55	0.71	0.84	0.95	1.00

Indicator	P5a	P5b	P5c	P5d	P5e	P5f
Weight	0.20	0.14	0.17	0.22	0.12	0.15

Dimension P6

Number	1	2	3	4	5
Eigenvalue	n.a.	n.a.	n.a.	n.a.	n.a.
Cum Prop	n.a.	n.a.	n.a.	n.a.	n.a.

Indicator	P6a	P6b	P6c	P6d	P6e
Weight	0.20	0.20	0.20	0.20	0.20

Dimension P7

Number	1	2	3	4	5	6
Eigenvalue	1.95	1.11	0.98	0.93	0.76	0.27
Cum Prop	0.32	0.51	0.67	0.83	0.96	1.00

Indicator	P7a	P7b	P7c	P7d	P7e	P7f
Weight	0.18	0.13	0.17	0.17	0.20	0.11

Dimension P8

Number	1	2	3	4
Eigenvalue	1.46	1.18	0.75	0.61
Cum Prop	0.36	0.66	0.85	1.00

Indicator	P8a	P8b	P8c	P8d
Weight	0.24	0.20	0.28	0.28

continued on next page

Table 2.2 continued

Number of principal components and implied weights: Dimensions

Number of principal components and implied weights: Overall

Number	1	2	3	4	5	6	7	8
Eigenvalue	2.52	1.81	1.20	0.93	0.64	0.36	0.31	0.23
Cum Prop	0.32	0.54	0.69	0.81	0.89	0.93	0.97	1.00

Indicator	P1	P2	P3	P4	P5	P6	P7	P8
Weight	0.11	0.13	0.13	0.12	0.13	0.11	0.14	0.13

Latin America

Number of principal components and implied weights: Dimensions

Dimension P1

Number	1	2	3	4
Eigenvalue	1.81	1.42	0.56	0.21
Cum Prop	0.45	0.81	0.95	1.00
Indicator	P1a	P1b	P1e	P1f
Weight	0.23	0.22	0.28	0.28

Dimension P2

Number	1	2	3	4	5
Eigenvalue	1.66	1.28	0.93	0.68	0.46
Cum Prop	0.33	0.59	0.77	0.91	1.00
Indicator	P2a	P2b	P2c	P2d	P2e
Weight	0.19	0.20	0.18	0.17	0.25

Dimension P3

Number	1	2	3	4	5
Eigenvalue	1.41	1.26	1.00	0.92	0.42
Cum Prop	0.28	0.53	0.73	0.92	1.00
Indicator	P3a	P3b	P3c	P3d	P3e
Weight	0.23	0.22	0.20	0.23	0.12

Dimension P4

Number	1	2	3	4	5
Eigenvalue	2.18	1.04	0.83	0.69	0.26
Cum Prop	0.44	0.64	0.81	0.95	1.00
Indicator	P4a	P4b	P4c	P4d	P4e
Weight	0.10	0.19	0.24	0.24	0.22

Dimension P5

Number	1	2	3	4	5	6
Eigenvalue	1.58	1.51	1.05	0.77	0.66	0.44
Cum Prop	0.26	0.51	0.69	0.82	0.93	1.00
Indicator	P5a	P5b	P5c	P5d	P5e	P5f
Weight	0.18	0.20	0.17	0.14	0.15	0.17

Dimension P6

Number	1	2	3	4	5
Eigenvalue	3.15	1.01	0.43	0.33	0.08
Cum Prop	0.63	0.83	0.92	0.98	1.00
Indicator	P6a	P6b	P6c	P6d	P6e
Weight	0.23	0.18	0.17	0.21	0.21

Dimension P7

Number	1	2	3	4	5	6
Eigenvalue	2.49	1.22	0.87	0.65	0.45	0.32
Cum Prop	0.42	0.62	0.76	0.87	0.95	1.00
Indicator	P7a	P7b	P7c	P7d	P7e	P7f
Weight	0.21	0.14	0.21	0.17	0.12	0.15

Dimension P8

Number	1	2	3	4
Eigenvalue	1.56	1.36	0.73	0.46
Cum Prop	0.39	0.73	0.88	1.00
Indicator	P8a	P8b	P8c	P8d
Weight	0.28	0.27	0.23	0.22

Number of principal components and implied weights: Overall

Number	1	2	3	4	5	6	7	8
Eigenvalue	2.03	1.60	1.21	1.13	0.75	0.51	0.44	0.33
Cum Prop	0.25	0.45	0.60	0.75	0.84	0.90	0.96	1.00

Indicator	P1	P2	P3	P4	P5	P6	P7	P8
Weight	0.12	0.09	0.14	0.13	0.12	0.14	0.13	

Africa

Number of principal components and implied weights: Dimensions

Dimension P1

Number	1	2	3	4
Eigenvalue	2.01	1.37	0.41	0.21
Cum Prop	0.50	0.84	0.95	1.00
Indicator	P1a	P1b	P1e	P1f
Weight	0.24	0.24	0.26	0.26

Dimension P2

Number	1	2	3	4	5
Eigenvalue	1.51	1.23	0.87	0.82	0.57
Cum Prop	0.30	0.55	0.72	0.89	1.00
Indicator	P2a	P2b	P2c	P2d	P2e
Weight	0.19	0.20	0.13	0.24	0.24

Dimension P3

Number	1	2	3	4	5
Eigenvalue	1.78	1.13	0.93	0.63	0.53
Cum Prop	0.36	0.58	0.77	0.89	1.00
Indicator	P3a	P3b	P3c	P3d	P3e
Weight	0.20	0.17	0.25	0.19	0.18

Dimension P4

Number	1	2	3	4	5
Eigenvalue	2.19	1.07	0.89	0.57	0.29
Cum Prop	0.44	0.65	0.83	0.94	1.00
Indicator	P4a	P4b	P4c	P4d	P4e
Weight	0.16	0.20	0.23	0.21	0.21

continued on next page

Table 2.2 continued

Number of principal components and implied weights: Dimensions

Dimension P5
Number	1	2	3	4	5	6
Eigenvalue	1.87	1.41	1.06	0.71	0.58	0.36
Cum Prop	0.15	0.17	0.18	0.16	0.18	0.15
Indicator	P5a	P5b	P5c	P5d	P5e	P5f
Weight	0.14	0.17	0.19	0.15	0.18	0.15

Dimension P6
Number	1	2	3	4	5	6
Eigenvalue	2.47	1.02	0.84	0.44	0.23	0.20
Cum Prop	0.23	0.20	0.20	0.17	0.19	0.14
Indicator	P6a	P6b	P6c	P6d	P6e	P6f
Weight	0.23	0.20	0.20	0.17	0.20	0.14

Dimension P7
Number	1	2	3	4	5	6
Eigenvalue	2.77	1.07	0.94	0.56	0.46	0.20
Cum Prop	0.19	0.14	0.20	0.16	0.17	0.14
Indicator	P7a	P7b	P7c	P7d	P7e	P7f
Weight	0.19	0.14	0.20	0.16	0.17	0.14

Dimension P8
Number	1	2	3	4
Eigenvalue	1.59	1.07	0.86	0.48
Cum Prop	0.28	0.23	0.22	0.27
Indicator	P8a	P8b	P8c	P8d
Weight	0.25	0.26	0.23	0.26

Overall
Number	1	2	3	4	5	6	7	8
Eigenvalue	2.06	1.88	1.11	0.88	0.72	0.61	0.41	0.33
Cum Prop	0.26	0.49	0.63	0.74	0.83	0.91	0.96	1.00
Indicator	P1	P2	P3	P4	P5	P6	P7	P8
Weight	0.09	0.14	0.13	0.13	0.14	0.13	0.12	0.12

Middle East

Number of principal components and implied weights: Dimensions

Dimension P1
Number	1	2	3	4
Eigenvalue	2.19	1.13	0.54	0.14
Cum Prop	0.55	0.83	0.96	1.00
Indicator	P1a	P1b	P1e	P1f
Weight	0.22	0.22	0.28	0.28

Dimension P2
Number	1	2	3	4	5
Eigenvalue	2.40	0.96	0.77	0.53	0.34
Cum Prop	0.48	0.67	0.83	0.93	1.00
Indicator	P2a	P2b	P2c	P2d	P2e
Weight	0.17	0.22	0.13	0.18	0.30

Dimension P3
Number	1	2	3	4	5
Eigenvalue	1.57	1.39	0.99	0.56	0.48
Cum Prop	0.31	0.59	0.79	0.90	1.00
Indicator	P3a	P3b	P3c	P3d	P3e
Weight	0.23	0.17	0.18	0.21	0.20

Dimension P4
Number	1	2	3	4	5
Eigenvalue	3.09	0.98	0.48	0.37	0.08
Cum Prop	0.62	0.82	0.91	0.98	1.00
Indicator	P4a	P4b	P4c	P4d	P4e
Weight	0.16	0.20	0.22	0.21	0.21

Dimension P5
Number	1	2	3	4	5	6
Eigenvalue	1.97	1.55	1.09	0.61	0.47	0.31
Cum Prop	0.33	0.59	0.77	0.87	0.95	1.00
Indicator	P5a	P5b	P5c	P5d	P5e	P5f
Weight	0.17	0.14	0.18	0.18	0.19	0.15

Dimension P6
Number	1	2	3	4	5	6
Eigenvalue	2.43	1.32	0.81	0.32	0.23	0.13
Cum Prop	0.49	0.75	0.91	0.97	1.00	1.00
Indicator	P6a	P6b	P6c	P6d	P6e	P6f
Weight	0.24	0.22	0.21	0.17	0.17	0.15

Dimension P7
Number	1	2	3	4	5	6
Eigenvalue	3.19	1.05	0.91	0.51	0.22	0.13
Cum Prop	0.53	0.71	0.86	0.94	0.98	1.00
Indicator	P7a	P7b	P7c	P7d	P7e	P7f
Weight	0.19	0.16	0.18	0.17	0.14	0.16

Dimension P8
Number	1	2	3	4
Eigenvalue	2.03	1.08	0.82	0.07
Cum Prop	0.51	0.78	0.98	1.00
Indicator	P8a	P8b	P8c	P8d
Weight	0.19	0.21	0.30	0.30

Number of principal components and implied weights: Overall
Number	1	2	3	4	5	6	7	8
Eigenvalue	3.31	2.35	0.96	0.83	0.60	0.30	0.15	0.10
Cum Prop	0.41	0.71	0.83	0.90	0.94	0.97	0.99	1.00
Indicator	P1	P2	P3	P4	P5	P6	P7	P8
Weight	0.11	0.12	0.10	0.13	0.14	0.14	0.12	0.14

Note: The "Cum Prop" row reports the cumulated proportion of total variation in the data accounted for by the principal components. The values highlighted in red are the principal components chosen for the aggregation.

Source: Asian Development Bank. Asia-Pacific Regional Cooperation and Integration Index Database. https://aric.adb.org/database/arcii (accessed November 2023).

CHAPTER 3
Regional Integration Index Construction and Trends

To the extent that globalization and regionalization are connected processes, a comparable measure of regional economic integration can be a good guide for determining how regional and global linkages are coupled and complement each other. Regional cooperation and integration describes the process in which neighboring economies expand linkages and coordinate policies to attain common objectives. In Asia and the Pacific, progress in this regard has been pivotal to improving economic growth, social inclusion, tackling poverty, and enhancing institutional stability. The Global Integration Index (GII) was constructed in parallel with the Regional Integration Index described in Chapter 2 to create a comparable metric for how economies fare in global and regional integration. This chapter provides an overview on the method used to create the RII and discusses the main trends revealed by the estimates.

3.1 Index Construction

The RII follows the same methodology and framework as the GII. While the foundations are similar, some data and methodological differences between the two indexes should be pointed out. First, the indicators in the RII are defined in terms of regional values, marked by the designator "(regional)" wherever applicable in Table 2.1. Second, the indicators on services exports (P1c) and services imports (P1d) are not included because data for regional values are not available. Finally, both the Kaiser criterion and Joliffe criterion used in principal component analysis are applied for all cases except for the institutional arrangements dimension in the European Union (EU) and all dimensions in North America.[1] To estimate the RII, a principal component analysis is completed separately for each region to capture idiosyncratic regional features. Accordingly, the number of principal components and implied weights by indicator and dimension vary between regions.[2]

3.2 Comparing the Regional Integration Index with the ARCII

While the RII presented in this report yields many similarities with ADB's Asia-Pacific Regional Cooperation and Integration Index (ARCII), some important differences need to be highlighted. Introduced in 2021, the ARCII baseline was expanded from six to eight dimensions to better capture the evolving regional integration landscape.

---

[1]   The EU has established plurilateral agreements among its member economies regarding free trade agreements (FTAs). Hence, the FTA indicator (P6a) in the regional index for the EU marks a score of 1 across all EU economies, yielding no cross-correlation to other indicators in the institutional arrangements dimension. As principal components analysis is inapplicable in this case, the composite index for the institutional arrangement dimension in the EU is produced by averaging the member indicators equally (i.e., equal weighting). In North America, equal weighting is used for aggregation in constructing dimensional indexes and the overall RII as there are only two economies in region.

[2]   For illustration, Asia and the Pacific attributes the highest weight for the infrastructure and connectivity dimension (0.137), and the lowest weight on environmental cooperation dimension (0.106).

Both ARCII and the GII use an eight-dimension framework that allows for a comprehensive tracking of regional integration progress. While ARCII is comprehensive in scope, it can be limited by data availability in some indicators. By construction, some ARCII indicators can also be less comparable with a global index. In contrast, the new RII facilitates comparability between regional and global integration. The new RII and the ARCII present similar features for economy coverage and the number of dimensions and indicators included in their frameworks (Table 3.1). The most distinct differences are the denominator and normalization method used in certain indicators. Different denominators (e.g., GDP, population) in the RII is a key feature, as their use ensures comparability with the GII.[3]

Table 3.1: Comparison between the ARCII and RII Frameworks

	ARCII	RII
Economy coverage	• 6 regions (Asia and the Pacific, the EU, Latin America, Africa, North America, and the Middle East) • 173 economies	
Dimensions and indicator coverage	• 8 dimensions • 41 indicators	
Denominator choice	• World totals	• GDP or population in some indicators
Normalization method	Panel min-max normalization	
Methodology	• PCA conducted to for the RII • IEII and EEII averaged to derive the Global Economic Integration Index	• PCA conducted for GII and RII. • No corresponding computation for measuring extraregional integration

EU = European Union, EEII = Extraregional Economic Integration Index, GDP = gross domestic product, GII = Global Integration Index, IEII = Intraregional Economic Integration Index, PCA = principal components analysis, RII = Regional Integration Index.

Source: ADB. 2021. *Asia-Pacific Regional Cooperation and Integration Index: Enhanced Framework, Analysis and Applications.* Manila.

While ARCII estimates tend to be higher, trends between the RII and the ARCII are similar. A comparison of both regional integration indexes confirms that the EU is the best performing region in both frameworks, while Africa and Latin America have the lowest estimates (Figure 3.1). Furthermore, RII and ARCII show a positive correlation across most dimensions (Figure 3.2). This underlines strong co-movements between the two indexes, where economies with a high score in the overall RII also score highly in the ARCII. The two indexes report a high correlation in institutional arrangements, whereas the correlation in trade and investment and people and social integration is lower—and mostly explained by differences in the denominator used for certain indicators.[4]

---

[3]   The RII framework applies GDP as the denominator for the indicators on goods exports and imports (trade and investment dimension), and total population for indicators on tourism, migration, and trademark applications (people and social integration dimension). In contrast, the ARCII framework utilizes world total flows as denominator.

[4]   A detailed discussion on the advantages and disadvantages of the denominator choice (i.e., GDP or population; world totals) is provided in Chapter 4 of ADB (2021).

Figure 3.1: Comparison between the ARCII and the RII

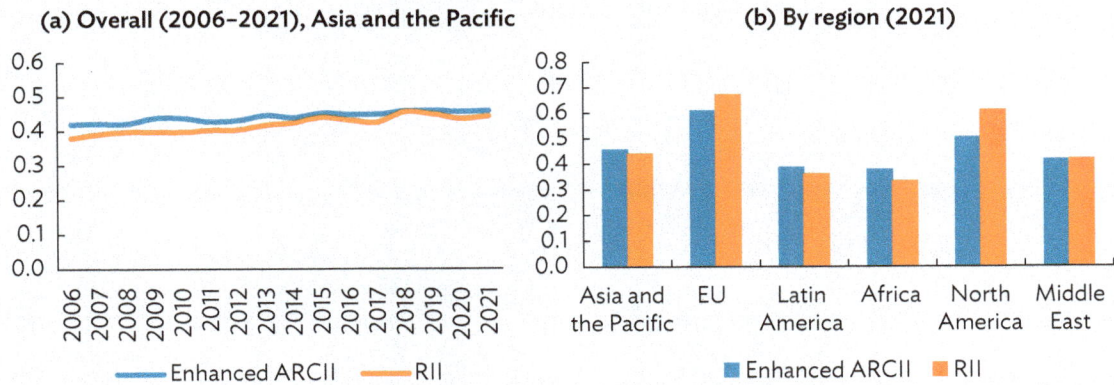

(a) Overall (2006–2021), Asia and the Pacific

(b) By region (2021)

Enhanced ARCII ———— RII

ARCII = Asia-Pacific Regional Cooperation and Integration Index, EU = European Union, RII = Regional Integration Index.

Source: ADB calculations using data from ADB. Asia-Pacific Regional Cooperation and Integration Index Database. https://aric.adb.org/database/arcii (accessed November 2023).

Figure 3.2: Correlation between the RII and the ARCII

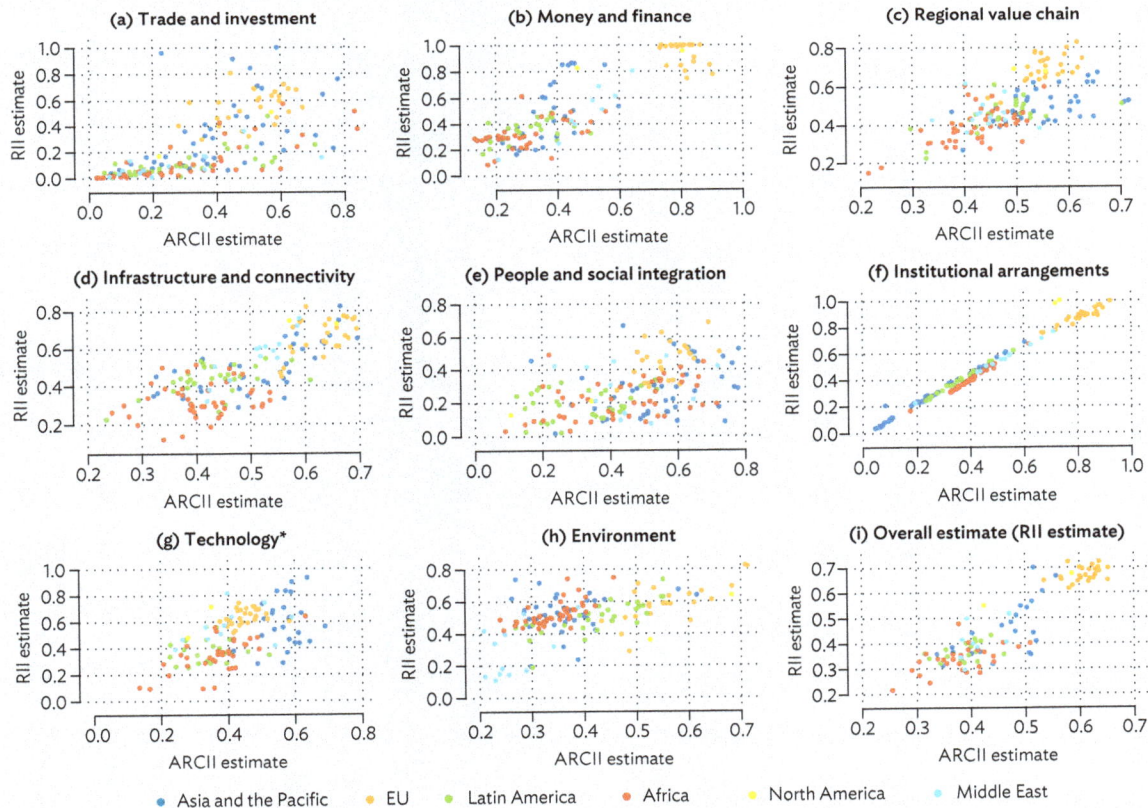

(a) Trade and investment
(b) Money and finance
(c) Regional value chain
(d) Infrastructure and connectivity
(e) People and social integration
(f) Institutional arrangements
(g) Technology*
(h) Environment
(i) Overall estimate (RII estimate)

● Asia and the Pacific ● EU ● Latin America ● Africa ● North America ● Middle East

ARCII = Asia-Pacific Regional Cooperation and Integration Index, EU = European Union, RII = Regional Integration Index, Technology* = Technology and digital connectivity.

Source: ADB calculations using data from ADB. Asia-Pacific Regional Cooperation and Integration Index Database. https://aric.adb.org/database/arcii (accessed November 2023).

3.3 Trends in Regional Integration: Evidence from the RII

Context-Based Discussion

Recent events such as the trade war between the People's Republic of China (PRC) and the United States (US), the coronavirus disease (COVID-19) pandemic, and the Russian invasion of Ukraine have impacted globalization and led to supply chain disruptions, macroeconomic imbalances, and a retrenchment of global connections. While the trend toward regionalization is less clear, deglobalization—or the process where economies become more isolated—could result in increased integration within regional partners.[5]

Some evidence suggests that the intensification of regional linkages had already started in some regions before the COVID-19 pandemic. This is particularly true for the EU and Asia and the Pacific where intraregional trade in goods account for more than half of the total (Figure 3.3). Other regionalization indicators, such as the nearshoring index (an indicator of the importance of regional value chains) show that regional linkages in Asia gradually increased up until the COVID-19 pandemic.

Figure 3.3: Trends in Intraregional Flows, 2021
(% of total)

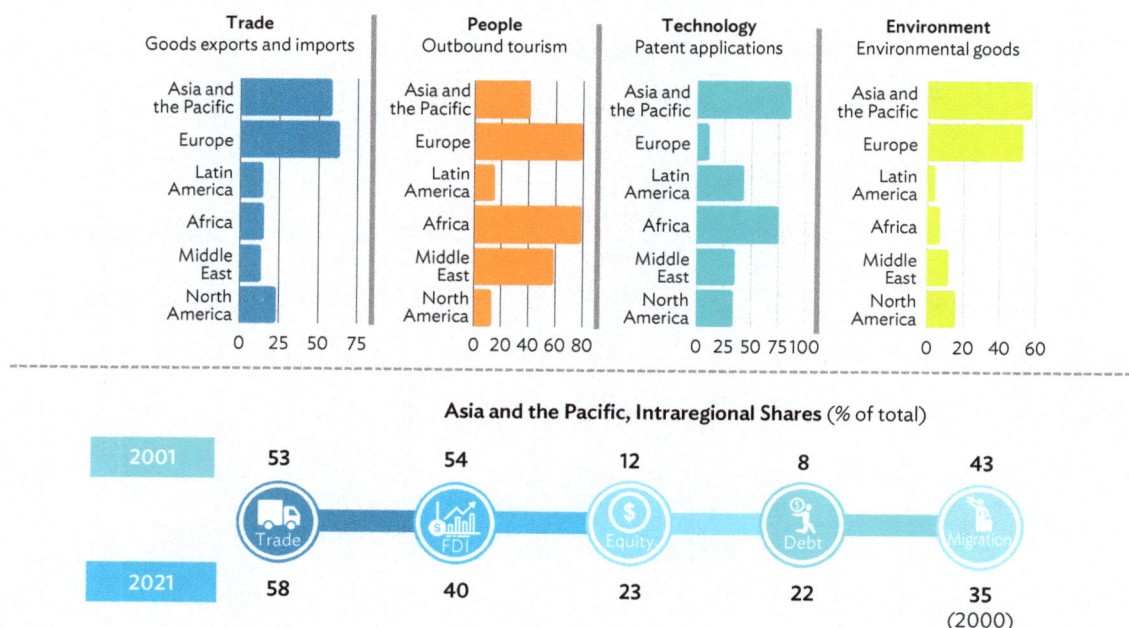

Equity = equity asset holdings (stock data), FDI = foreign direct investment (flows data), Debt = debt asset holdings (stock data).

Note: Migration and tourism are based on outbound data. Where 2021 data are not available, the latest year for available data is indicated in parentheses.

Sources: ADB calculations using data from Association of Southeast Asian Nations Secretariat; International Monetary Fund; Organisation for Economic Co-operation and Development; United Nations Conference on Trade and Development; United Nations Department of Economic and Social Affairs, Population Division; United Nations World Tourism Organization; World Bank; and national sources (all accessed May 2023).

---

[5]   A focused discussion on deglobalization is provided in Box 3.1.

Estimates from the RII show a general improvement in regional integration. Most economies in Asia and the Pacific, Latin America, Africa, and the Middle East experienced an improvement in regional integration between 2006 and 2021, with a few exceptions (Annex 3b). Trends in the EU region tend to be more mixed, with regional integration in some economies showing a small decrease. It is worth noting, however, that RII estimates for EU economies have been consistently higher than most other regions. High performers in regional integration are not restricted to Europe. Singapore and Malaysia are among economies in Asia and the Pacific that also report high estimates for regional integration. This is partly explained by their important trade, investment, and institutional linkages. Besides the US, the main trading partners of these three economies are all Asian economies.[6]

Box 3.1: Slowbalization, Newbalization, and the Narratives of Deglobalization

The varying benefits of globalization, if not its outright welfare costs, have led policymakers to debate the notion of deglobalization. This has been defined as "a movement toward a less connected world, characterized by powerful nation states, local solutions, and border controls rather than global institutions, treaties, and free movement" (Kornprobst and Wallace 2022). As stressed in Chapter 4, the implication of globalization on inequality and poverty, particularly in developing economies, is a contentious topic (Elliott, Kar, and Richardson 2002). Today, concerns about the impact of globalization on climate change, workers' rights or intellectual property, among others, also resonate in current discussions.

Globalization's skeptics point out that under certain conditions integration has yielded unwanted outcomes on climate, poverty, inequality, and inclusiveness. The debates touch an array of globalization modalities, from free trade agreements, cross-border investment and financial flows, to the lending practices of multilateral financial institutions, among others.

Recent geopolitical tensions have favored more inward-looking economic policies, generated by political uncertainty and skepticism toward global processes and institutions (Manfredi-Sánchez 2021). However, the evidence in favor or against deglobalization as a trend is mixed. For some, deglobalization was already happening before relations among economic behemoths soured, and was demonstrated by decreasing flows of merchandize, capital, and people and the intensity of strategic competition between the People's Republic of China and the United States (García-Herrero 2020). For others, deglobalization has manifested more clearly in developed than in developing economies (Kim, Li, and Lee 2020).

At the same time, the slowdown in globalization may not necessarily be an indication of deglobalization (Antràs 2020). The term "slowbalization" has been coined to describe the slowing growth in cross-border flows and movement of people after the global financial crisis in 2008–2009 (Canuto 2022). Strong economic interdependence also suggests that while political deglobalization could be happening, economic deglobalization is not (Kleintop 2022).

Regardless of its current state, deglobalization risks cannot be discounted completely. Apart from impacts on economic growth, employment, cross-border flows, economic inclusion, inequality, and poverty, technology and digital standards are expected to be significantly affected by deglobalization. Indeed, globalization has boosted the adoption of technology globally which has in turn facilitated the flow of knowledge, ideas, and innovation (Aslam et al. 2018). It has also created new avenues to trade and investment through the internationalization of small and medium-sized enterprises, the expansion of digital services trade and online working, among other trends. These new channels have been referred as "newbalization." A shift toward deglobalization could also slow down technological progress and entail a redistribution of the benefits of globalization (Kalish 2022).

Source: Asian Development Bank.

---

[6] Information obtained from the World Integrated Trade Solution (WITS) of the World Bank. https://wits.worldbank.org/.

Results by Region and Income Group

Regional integration has improved across income groups, although high-income economies are more integrated. Following the trend in global economic integration, high-income economies also tend to be the most regionally integrated (Figure 3.4, panel a). This trend may be driven by EU economies which, together with the US and Canada, are in the high-income group. The upper-middle, lower-middle, and low-income groups reported lower estimates and more moderate growth in regional integration from 2006 to 2021. The distribution of RII estimates also suggests that most of the economies belonging to the low-income group have low scores (Figure 3.4, panel b). Distribution of scores for upper and lower middle-income economies is less concentrated, suggesting higher variation in regional integration among middle-income economies. In contrast to GII scores, the range for RII estimates in high-income economies is also wide.

Figure 3.4: Regional Integration Index, by Income Level

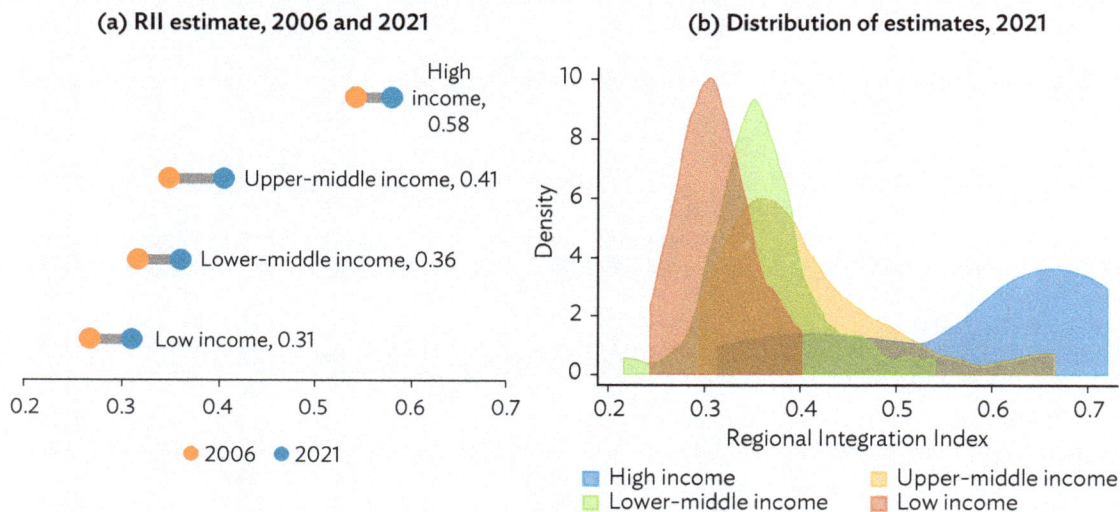

(a) RII estimate, 2006 and 2021

High income, 0.58

Upper-middle income, 0.41

Lower-middle income, 0.36

Low income, 0.31

● 2006 ● 2021

(b) Distribution of estimates, 2021

Regional Integration Index

■ High income   ■ Upper-middle income
■ Lower-middle income   ■ Low income

Sources: ADB calculations using data from ADB. Asia-Pacific Regional Cooperation and Integration Index Database. https://aric.adb.org/database/arcii; World Bank. World Development Indicators. https://databank.worldbank.org/source/world-developmentindicators (all accessed November 2023).

By region, regional integration has strengthened over time. As with global integration, regional integration improved from 2006 to 2021 across all economies (Figure 3.5). While regional averages mask significant differences in regional integration across economies, the trend is stable over time. The downturns identified for the GII (2008–2009, 2011–2012, 2015–2016, and 2019–2020) are also observed for regional integration, with some exceptions. For example, the euro area debt crisis in 2011 and 2012 had less effect on regional integration in some developing regions (e.g., Latin America, and the Middle East).

By region, the EU has the deepest regional integration. Consistent with ARCII measures, the EU is the most integrated region in most dimensions. Asia and the Pacific and the Middle East follow the EU, with the Middle East reflecting progress on regional cooperation through the Gulf Cooperation Council and other initiatives. Africa is the least integrated region, with several economies more integrated globally than regionally. Low RII estimates can also entail stronger extraregional linkages because of regional markets being less developed or some dimensions having narrower scope for regional integration than others. For Africa, this is reflected by the lack of trade and production complementarities and institutional arrangements (African Union 2021). Regional integration in Asian economies is more wide-ranging than in other regions. Economy-level performance suggests a large variation across Asia and the Pacific, from low estimates (0.29 in Tajikistan) to very high estimates (0.70 in Singapore) (Figure 3.5, panel b). In contrast, regional integration estimates for economies in Africa, the EU, and Latin America are more concentrated.

Figure 3.5: Regional Integration Index, by Region

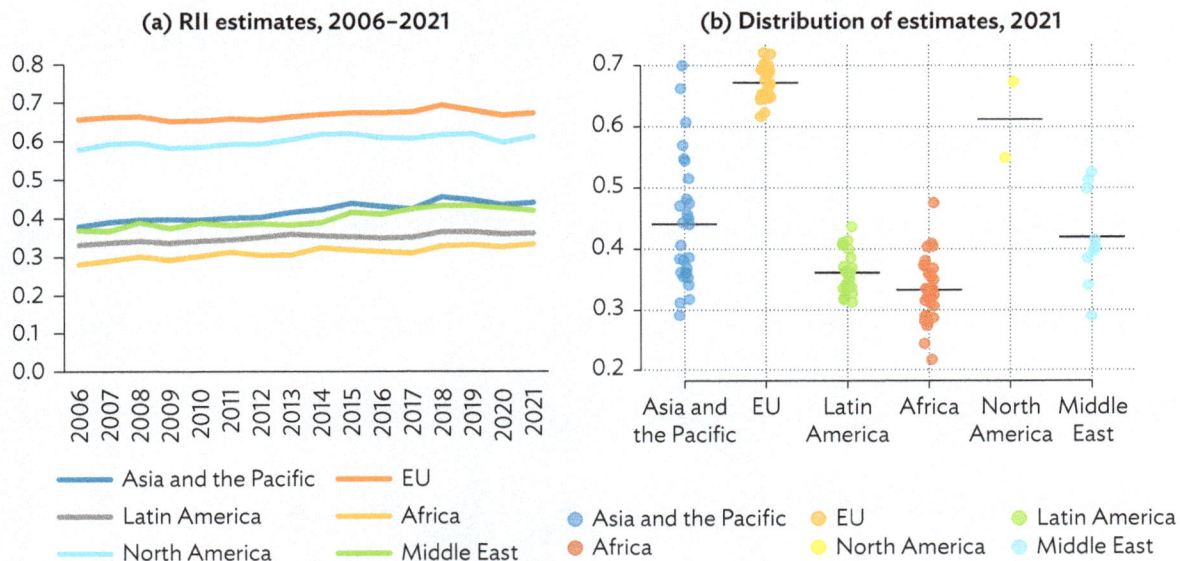

(a) RII estimates, 2006–2021

(b) Distribution of estimates, 2021

Asia and the Pacific — EU — Latin America — Africa — North America — Middle East

Asia and the Pacific • EU • Latin America • Africa • North America • Middle East

EU = European Union, RII = Regional Integration Index.

Source: ADB calculations using data from ADB. Asia-Pacific Regional Cooperation and Integration Index Database. https://aric.adb.org/database/arcii (accessed November 2023).

Regional integration estimates highlight regional differences in most dimensions. Similarly to the GII, the RII shows persistent heterogeneity between regions and across dimensions. The EU is the best performing region in several dimensions, notably in money and finance and institutional arrangements (Figure 3.6). High regional estimates for the EU can be attributed to factors that include the establishment of the EU's single market to the adoption of a common monetary policy and currency. Asia and the Pacific performed similarly to the EU in trade and investment, supported by increasing intraregional trade and trade and investment liberalization reforms. Whereas most dimensions highlight regional differences, these are relatively small for environmental cooperation. The Middle East is least regionally integrated in environmental cooperation, mirroring its position in the GII.

Within Asia subregions, Southeast Asia and East Asia are the most integrated with Asia and the Pacific. These two subregions are well integrated in nearly all dimensions, facilitated by subregional cooperation efforts through key action plans, trade facilitation, investment, and strengthening supply chains (ADB 2021). The ASEAN Free Trade Area program, established in the 1990s, and similar programs laid the foundation for a more comprehensive regional integration plan for Southeast Asia (Dent 2017). The performance of Southeast Asia and East Asia also underscores the disparities with other subregions, in particular South Asia and Central Asia (Figure 3.7). These two subregions not only report lower RII estimates in infrastructure and connectivity, money and finance, and institutional integration, but also experienced overall improvement in regional integration from 2006 to 2021. These results are consistent with the ARCII and highlight that these regions have made slow but important progress in regional cooperation over the past 2 decades.

Figure 3.6: Dimensions of the Regional Integration Index, by Region

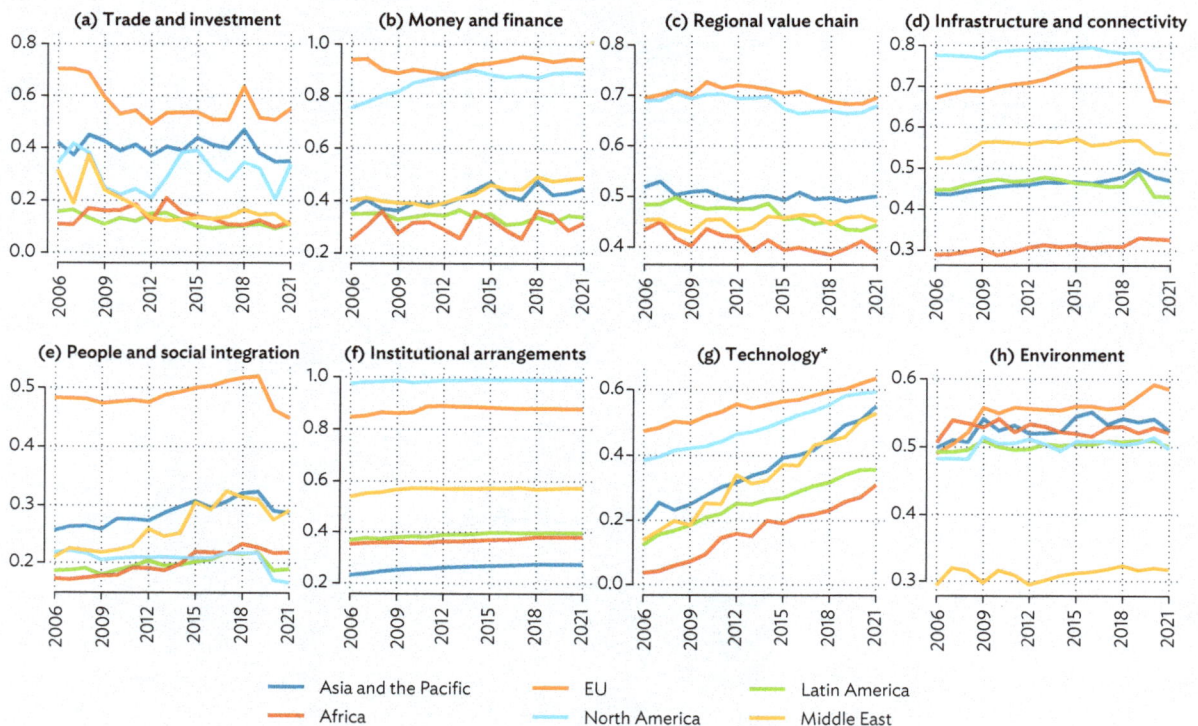

EU = European Union, Technology* = technology and digital connectivity.

Source: ADB calculations using data from ADB. Asia-Pacific Regional Cooperation and Integration Index Database. https://aric.adb.org/database/arcii (accessed November 2023).

By subregional initiative, Southeast Asian economies are the most integrated with the rest of the region. This is the case for Indonesia–Malaysia–Thailand Growth Triangle, closely followed by Brunei Darussalam–Indonesia–Malaysia–Philippines East ASEAN Growth Area, Association of Southeast Asian Nations, and the Greater Mekong Subregion Economic Cooperation Program, which includes mainly Southeast Asian economies (Figure 3.8). The large gaps between these and the other subregional initiatives became more pronounced in 2021. The Central Asia Regional Economic Cooperation Program, South Asian Association for Regional Cooperation, and South Asia Subregional Economic Cooperation have similar regional integration estimates in 2021 and are also the least integrated of the initiatives. However, all three registered improvements from 2006 to 2021. Despite being among the least regionally integrated, the Central Asia Regional Economic Cooperation Program posted the biggest improvement in regional integration among all subregional initiatives between 2006 and 2021.

Figure 3.7: Dimensions of the Regional Integration Index, by Asian Subregion

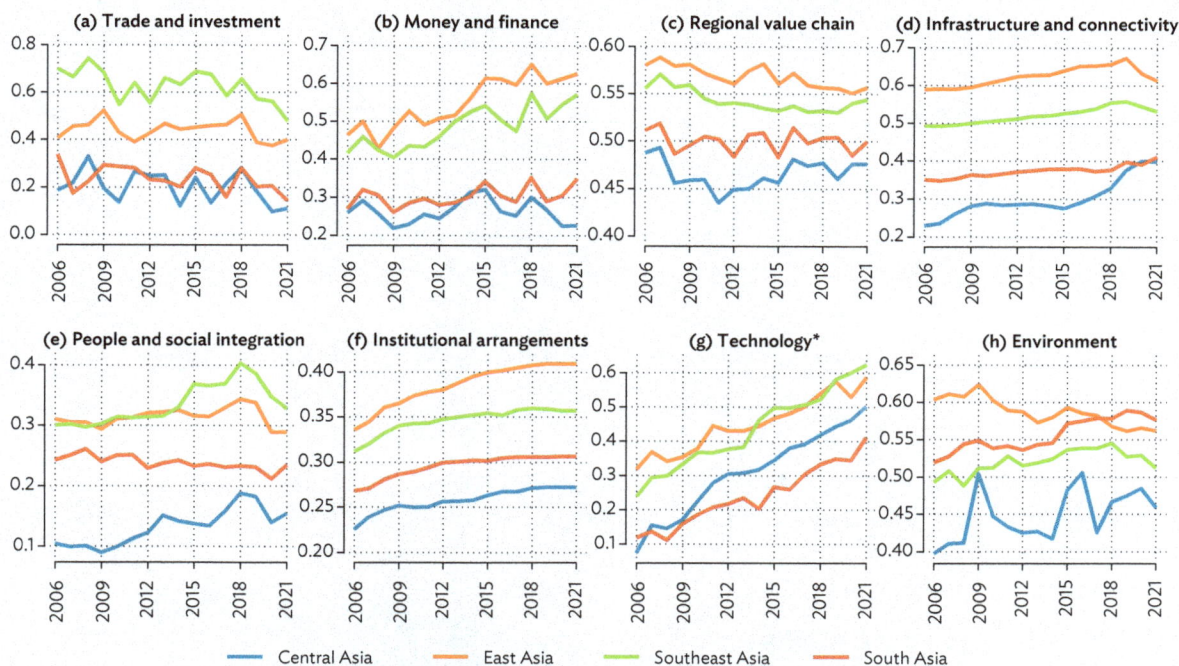

Technology* = technology and digital connectivity.

Note: The estimates represent integration of the subregion with Asia and the Pacific.

Source: ADB calculations using data from ADB. Asia-Pacific Regional Cooperation and Integration Index Database. https://aric.adb.org/database/arcii (accessed November 2023).

Figure 3.8: Regional Integration Index, by Subregional Initiative

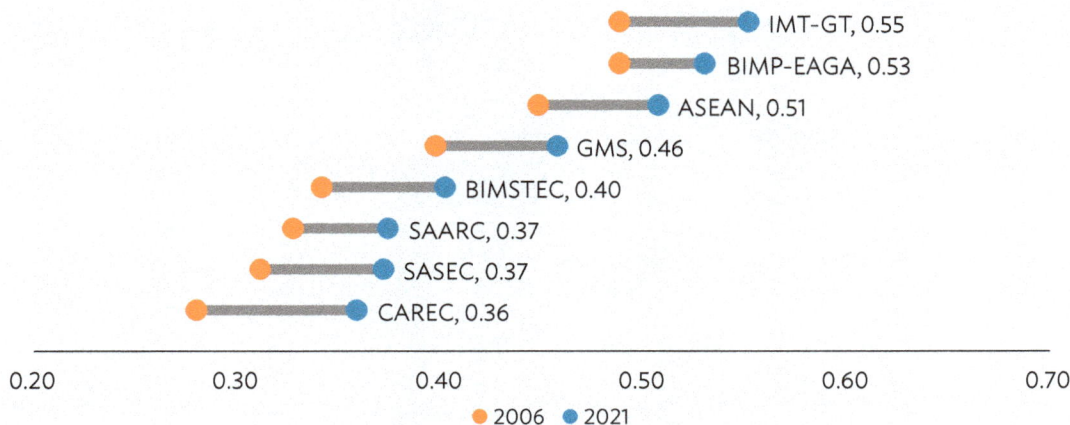

BIMP-EAGA = Brunei Darussalam–Indonesia–Malaysia–Philippines East ASEAN Growth Area, BIMSTEC = Bay of Bengal Initiative for Multi-Sectoral Technical and Economic Cooperation, IMT-GT = Indonesia–Malaysia–Thailand Growth Triangle, SAARC = South Asian Association for Regional Cooperation.

Source: ADB. Asia-Pacific Regional Cooperation and Integration Index Database. https://aric.adb.org/database/arcii (accessed November 2023).

Box 3.2: COVID-19 and Its Impact on Regional and Extraregional Trade and Investment

Trade

The coronavirus disease (COVID-19) pandemic affected global and regional trade dramatically, due to the dampening of global demand from cross-border restrictions and logistical disruptions (UNCTAD 2022). In 2020, global trade contracted by about 7% compared to 2019. For Asia and the Pacific, trade decreased by 4.6%, mainly in the first half of the year. It started to recover in the second half of 2020, followed by a strong rebound in 2021, with a 24.1% increase in global trade over pre-pandemic levels (Figure 3.2.1). Strong government monetary and fiscal support, vaccination programs, and the early success of pandemic-control measures in the region aided the recovery (WTO 2021, AEIR 2022).

Figure 3.2.1: Trend in Merchandise Trade, Asia and the Pacific ($ billion)

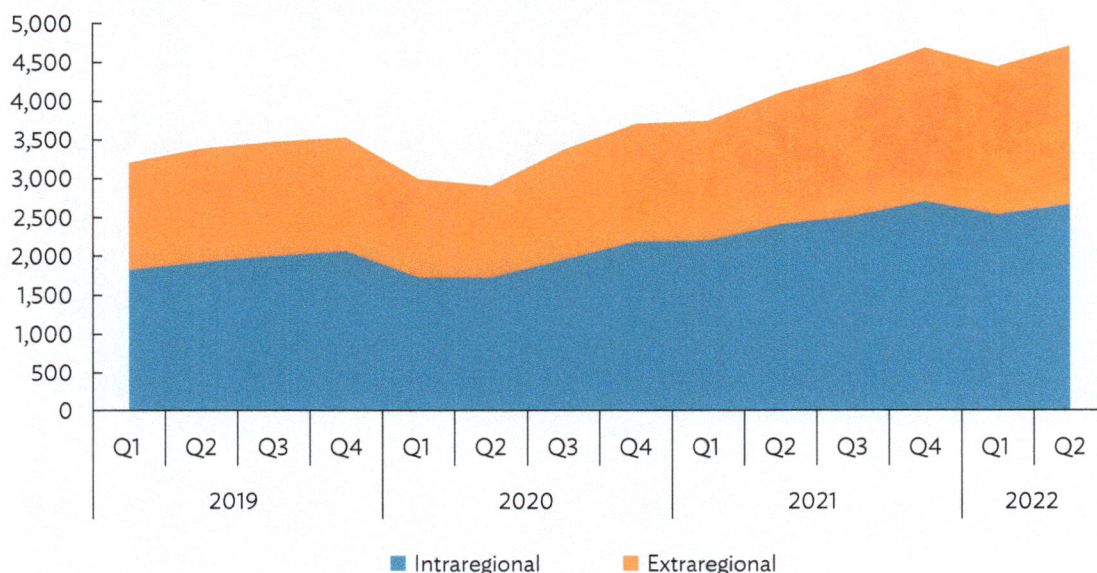

Q = quarter.

Source: International Monetary Fund. Direction of Trade Statistics. https://www.imf.org/en/Data (accessed October 2022).

A glance at regional trends in merchandise exports also highlights the varying effects of the pandemic. In terms of total trade, the adverse effects were less prominent in Asia and the Pacific than in other regions (Figure 3.2.2). For instance, the share of exports to GDP between 2019 and 2020 remained steady for Asia and the Pacific, while most other regions experienced contractions (Figure 3.2.2, panel a). Intraregional exports contracted during the same period, although recovered sharply in 2021. The recovery may have been partly driven by growth in exports from the People's Republic of China, which was faster than for other big economies in the second quarter of 2020 and early 2021 (OECD 2022).

Foreign direct investment

In comparison to trade, the pandemic affected foreign direct investment (FDI) more, as global FDI flows plummeted by 35%, in 2020 (UNCTAD 2021). Pandemic-related responses (e.g., lockdowns, social distancing) raised the operational costs of multinationals, and companies attempted to lessen their reliance on foreign affiliates to diversify risks from such responses (Lee and Park 2020; Hayakawa, Lee, and Park 2022). In contrast to global trends, FDI weakened moderately in Asia in the Pacific by a moderate 1.3% in 2020 (ADB 2022), mostly driven by a 38% dip in greenfield investment, but

continued on next page

Box 3.2 *continued*

cushioned by a 74.1% increase in merger and acquisition deals (Figure 3.2.3). Both global and intraregional flows show that FDI inflows to Asia and the Pacific were weaker due to the pandemic, with global inflows down 51% and intraregional flows decreasing by 66% between 2019 and 2020.

Figure 3.2.2: Trend in Merchandise Exports, by Region

(a) Global exports over GDP (%)

(b) Regional exports over GDP (%)

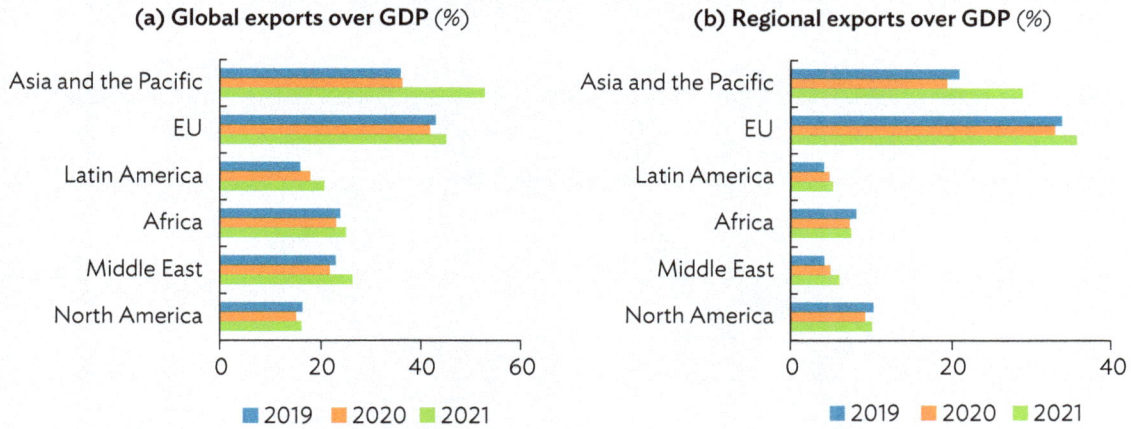

EU = European Union, GDP = gross domestic product.

Sources: International Monetary Fund. Direction of Trade Statistics. https://www.imf.org/en/Data; World Bank. World Development Indicators. https://databank.worldbank.org/source/world-developmentindicators (all accessed October 2022).

Figure 3.2.3: Inward FDI Flows, Asia and the Pacific ($ billion)

FDI = foreign direct investment, M&A = merger and acquisition, Q = quarter.

Sources: ADB calculations using data from Bureau van Dijk. Zephyr M&A Database; and Financial Times. fDi Markets (both accessed October 2022).

continued on next page

Box 3.2 *continued*

Figure 3.2.4: Trends in FDI Inflows, by Region

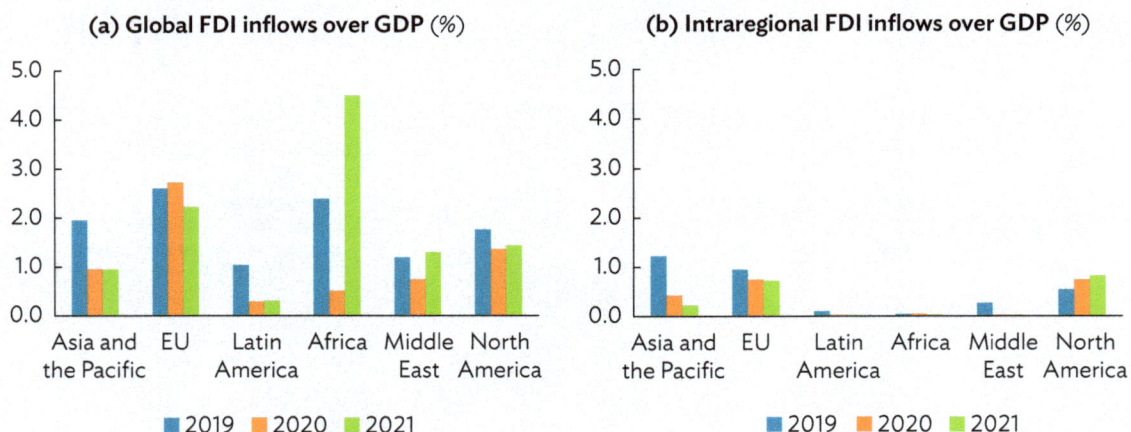

(a) Global FDI inflows over GDP (%)

2019 ■ 2020 ■ 2021

(b) Intraregional FDI inflows over GDP (%)

2019 ■ 2020 ■ 2021

EU = European Union, FDI = foreign direct investment, GDP = gross domestic product.

Sources: ADB calculations using data from Bureau van Dijk. Zephyr M&A Database; Financial Times. fDi Markets; World Bank. World Development Indicators. https://databank.worldbank.org/source/world-developmentindicators (all accessed October 2022).

References

Asian Development Bank (ADB). 2021. *Asia-Pacific Regional Cooperation and Integration Index: Enhanced Framework, Analysis and Applications.* Manila. http://dx.doi.org/10.22617/TCS210342-2.

———. 2022. *Asian Economic Integration Report 2022: Advancing Digital Services Trade in Asia and the Pacific.* Manila. https://dx.doi.org/10.22617/TCS220041-2.

African Union. 2021. *African Integration Report 2021: Putting Free Movement of Persons at the Centre of Continental Integration.* Addis Ababa. https://au.int/en/documents/african-integration-report-2021.

Aslam, A., J. Eugster, G. Ho, F. Jaumotte, C. Osorio-Buitron, and R. Piazza. 2018. Globalization Helps Spread Knowledge and Technology Across Borders. International Monetary Fund *Blog*, 9 April. https://www.imf.org/en/Blogs/Articles/2018/04/09/globalization-helps-spread-knowledge-and-technology-across-borders.

Canuto, O. 2022. *Slowbalization, Newbalization, Not Deglobalization.* Policy Center for the New South. 1 June. https://www.policycenter.ma/publications/slowbalization-newbalizationnot-deglobalization (accessed 13 December 2022).

Dent, C. M. 2017. East Asian Integration towards an East Asian Economic Community. *ADBI Working Paper Series. No. 665.* Tokyo: Asian Development Bank Institute. https://www.adb.org/sites/default/files/publication/228896/adbi-wp665.pdf.

Elliott, K. A., D. Kar, and J. D. Richardson. 2004. Assessing Globalization's Critics: "Talkers Are No Good Doers?" In R. E. Baldwin and A. Winters, eds. *Challenges to Globalization: Analyzing the Economics.* pp. 17-62. University of Chicago Press. http://www.nber.org/chapters/c9532.

Hayakawa, K., H-H. Lee, and C-Y. Park. 2022. The Effect of COVID-19 on Foreign Direct Investment. *ADB Economics Working Paper Series.* No. 653. Manila: ADB. https://dx.doi.org/10.2139/ssrn.4060417.

Kalish, I. 2022. Economic Brief: How Supply Chains Could Adapt to Deglobalization. *WSJ-CFO Journal.* https://deloitte.wsj.com/articles/economic-brief-how-supply-chainscould-adapt-to-deglobalization-01648666628 (accessed 30 March 2022).

Kleintop, J. 2022. *Deglobalization Is Political, Not Economic.* Charles Schwab & Co. 11 April. https://www.schwab.com/learn/story/deglobalization-is-political-not-economic (accessed 13 December 2022).

Kornprobst, M., and J. Wallace. 2022. What Is Deglobalization? *Chatham House Newsletter.* 12 October. https://www.chathamhouse.org/2021/10/what-deglobalization (accessed 13 December 2022).

Lee, H-H., and D. Park. 2020. *Post-COVID Asia: Deglobalization, Fourth Industrial Revolution, and Sustainable Development.* Singapore: World Scientific Publishing.

Manfredi-Sánchez, J-L. 2021. Deglobalization and Public Diplomacy. *International Journal of Communication.* 15. pp. 905–926. https://ijoc.org/index.php/ijoc/article/view/15379/3357.

Organisation for Economic Co-operation and Development. 2022. *International Trade during the COVID-19 Pandemic: Big Shifts and Uncertainty.* Paris. https://read.oecd-ilibrary.org/view/?ref=1129_1129345-casormobh7&title=International-trade-during-the-COVID-19-pandemic.

United Nations Conference on Trade and Development (UNCTAD). 2021. *World Investment Report 2021: Investing in Sustainable Recovery.* New York. https://unctad.org/system/files/official-document/wir2021_en.pdf.

———. 2022. *Impact of the COVID-19 Pandemic on Trade and Development: Lessons Learned.* New York. https://unctad.org/system/files/official-document/osg2022d1_en.pdf.

Annex 3.1a: Economy Estimates from the Global Integration Index

Asia and the Pacific

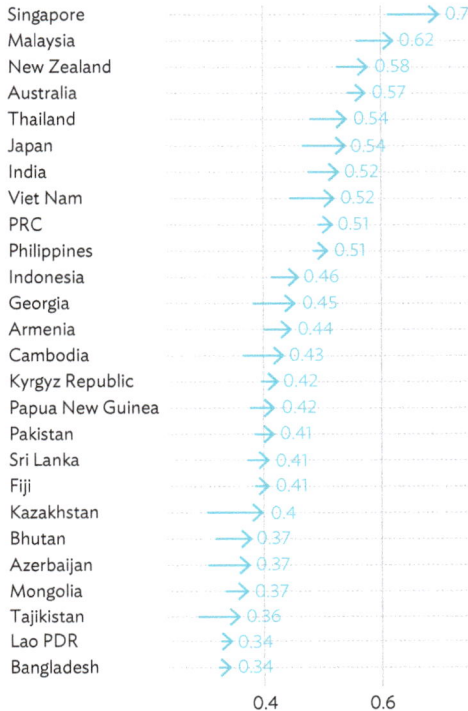

Economy	Value
Singapore	0.7
Malaysia	0.62
New Zealand	0.58
Australia	0.57
Thailand	0.54
Japan	0.54
India	0.52
Viet Nam	0.52
PRC	0.51
Philippines	0.51
Indonesia	0.46
Georgia	0.45
Armenia	0.44
Cambodia	0.43
Kyrgyz Republic	0.42
Papua New Guinea	0.42
Pakistan	0.41
Sri Lanka	0.41
Fiji	0.41
Kazakhstan	0.4
Bhutan	0.37
Azerbaijan	0.37
Mongolia	0.37
Tajikistan	0.36
Lao PDR	0.34
Bangladesh	0.34

Europe

Economy	Value
Netherlands	0.74
United Kingdom	0.72
Sweden	0.71
Belgium	0.7
Denmark	0.69
Germany	0.68
France	0.68
Finland	0.67
Austria	0.65
Spain	0.65
Hungary	0.65
Estonia	0.63
Italy	0.63
Lithuania	0.63
Ireland	0.63
Portugal	0.62
Cyprus	0.62
Malta	0.62
Latvia	0.61
Slovenia	0.61
Czech Republic	0.61
Bulgaria	0.59
Poland	0.59
Greece	0.58
Slovakia	0.58

Latin America

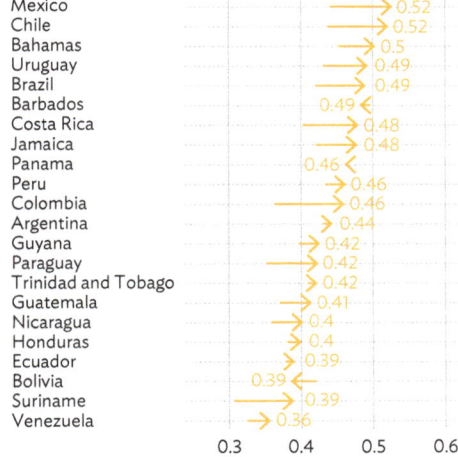

Economy	Value
Mexico	0.52
Chile	0.52
Bahamas	0.5
Uruguay	0.49
Brazil	0.49
Barbados	0.49
Costa Rica	0.48
Jamaica	0.48
Panama	0.46
Peru	0.46
Colombia	0.46
Argentina	0.44
Guyana	0.42
Paraguay	0.42
Trinidad and Tobago	0.42
Guatemala	0.41
Nicaragua	0.4
Honduras	0.4
Ecuador	0.39
Bolivia	0.39
Suriname	0.39
Venezuela	0.36

Africa

Economy	Value
Mauritius	0.57
South Africa	0.5
Morocco	0.5
Ghana	0.42
Senegal	0.42
Liberia	0.41
Algeria	0.4
Kenya	0.4
Nigeria	0.4
Cote d'Ivoire (Ivory Coast)	0.39
Lesotho	0.39
Botswana	0.38
Togo	0.38
Gambia	0.38
Cameroon	0.38
Mozambique	0.38
Zambia	0.37
Rwanda	0.36
Benin	0.36
Uganda	0.35
Guinea	0.34
Sierra Leone	0.34
Niger	0.34
Tanzania	0.34
Mali	0.34
Malawi	0.33
Angola	0.31
Chad	0.3
Madagascar	0.3

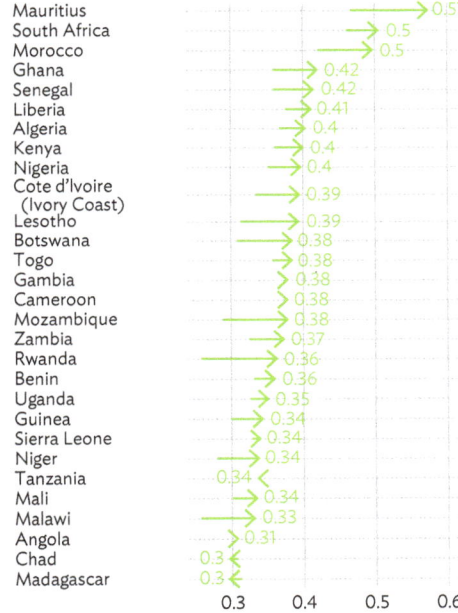

North America

Economy	Value
Canada	0.61
United States	0.58

Middle East

Economy	Value
United Arab Emirates	0.58
Bahrain	0.51
Jordan	0.51
Qatar	0.47
Kuwait	0.45
Lebanon	0.43
Saudi Arabia	0.41
Oman	0.4
Iran (Islamic Republic of)	0.35

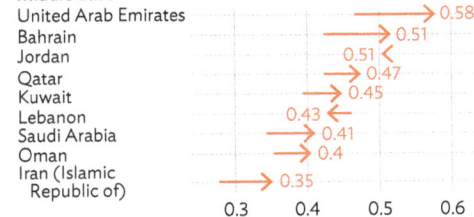

Lao PDR = Lao People's Democratic Republic, PRC = People's Republic of China.

Source: ADB calculations using data from ADB. Asia-Pacific Regional Cooperation and Integration Index Database. https://aric.adb.org/database/arcii (accessed November 2023).

Annex 3.2b: Economy Estimates from the Regional Integration Index

Asia and the Pacific

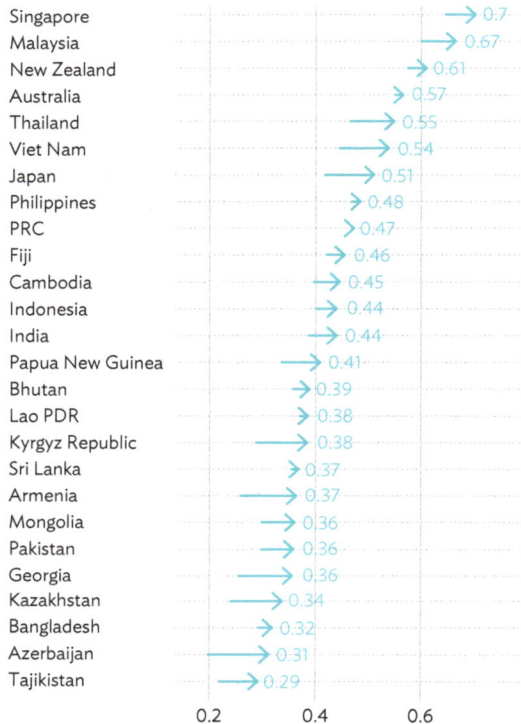

Economy	Value
Singapore	0.7
Malaysia	0.67
New Zealand	0.61
Australia	0.57
Thailand	0.55
Viet Nam	0.54
Japan	0.51
Philippines	0.48
PRC	0.47
Fiji	0.46
Cambodia	0.45
Indonesia	0.44
India	0.44
Papua New Guinea	0.41
Bhutan	0.39
Lao PDR	0.38
Kyrgyz Republic	0.38
Sri Lanka	0.37
Armenia	0.37
Mongolia	0.36
Pakistan	0.36
Georgia	0.36
Kazakhstan	0.34
Bangladesh	0.32
Azerbaijan	0.31
Tajikistan	0.29

Europe

Economy	Value
Denmark	0.72
Netherlands	0.72
Sweden	0.71
Hungary	0.7
Belgium	0.7
Austria	0.7
Estonia	0.69
Portugal	0.69
Lithuania	0.69
Finland	0.69
Latvia	0.68
Poland	0.67
Spain	0.67
Germany	0.66
United Kingdom	0.66
Slovenia	0.66
Czech Republic	0.66
Bulgaria	0.65
Malta	0.65
Slovakia	0.65
Cyprus	0.65
Greece	0.64
France	0.64
Ireland	0.63
Italy	0.62

Latin America

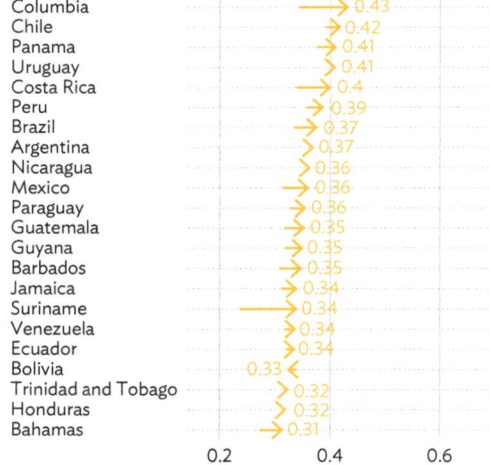

Economy	Value
Columbia	0.43
Chile	0.42
Panama	0.41
Uruguay	0.41
Costa Rica	0.4
Peru	0.39
Brazil	0.37
Argentina	0.37
Nicaragua	0.36
Mexico	0.36
Paraguay	0.36
Guatemala	0.35
Guyana	0.35
Barbados	0.35
Jamaica	0.34
Suriname	0.34
Venezuela	0.34
Ecuador	0.34
Bolivia	0.33
Trinidad and Tobago	0.32
Honduras	0.32
Bahamas	0.31

Africa

Economy	Value
Mauritius	0.48
South Africa	0.4
Togo	0.4
Botswana	0.38
Senegal	0.37
Cote d'Ivoire (Ivory Coast)	0.37
Rwanda	0.37
Morocco	0.36
Kenya	0.36
Benin	0.35
Mali	0.35
Cameroon	0.34
Lesotho	0.34
Ghana	0.34
Nigeria	0.33
Zambia	0.33
Guinea	0.32
Uganda	0.32
Sierra Leone	0.31
Gambia	0.31
Mozambique	0.31
Algeria	0.29
Niger	0.29
Tanzania	0.28
Malawi	0.28
Chad	0.28
Liberia	0.27
Madagascar	0.24
Angola	0.22

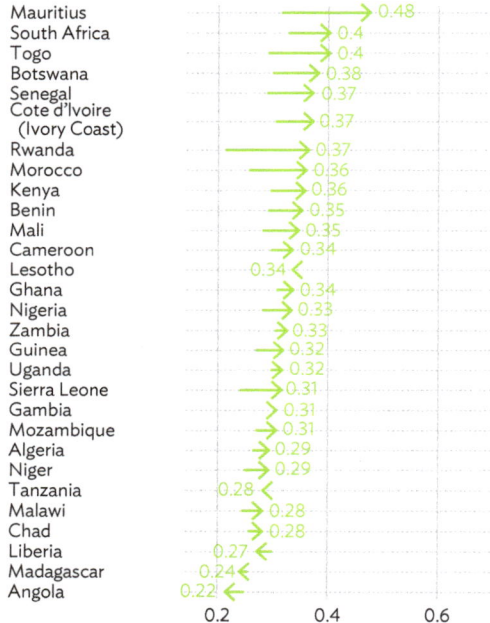

North America

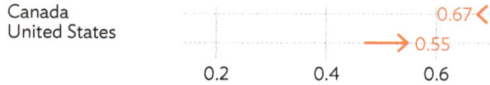

Economy	Value
Canada	0.67
United States	0.55

Middle East

Economy	Value
Bahrain	0.52
Jordan	0.52
United Arab Emirates	0.5
Lebanon	0.41
Oman	0.41
Qatar	0.4
Kuwait	0.39
Saudi Arabia	0.34
Iran (Islamic Republic of)	0.29

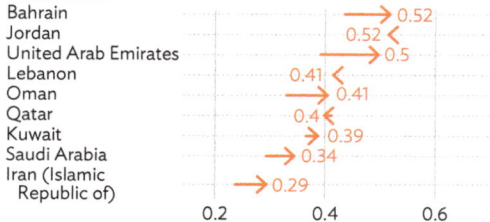

Lao PDR = Lao People's Democratic Republic, PRC = People's Republic of China.

Source: ADB calculations using data from ADB. Asia-Pacific Regional Cooperation and Integration Index Database. https://aric.adb.org/database/arcii (accessed November 2023).

CHAPTER 4
Understanding the Linkages Between Regional and Global Integration

The distributional impact of globalization is high on the policymaking agenda and related to current scenarios of deglobalization, international fragmentation, and regionalism. Recent economic shocks due to geopolitical tensions, the COVID-19 pandemic, and conflict have influenced debate over the reversal of cross-border flows and economic fragmentation. Regionalism has been considered an effective pillar of Asia's development story. It also has been presented as a stepping stone, if not an alternative, to globalization, stemming from the view that regional cooperation can provide better protection from potential global risks yet enable economies to realize benefits from foreign trade. In the same spirit, the effect of global and regional integration on development outcomes appears less straightforward. Global and regional integration and economic growth are reinforcing in general, but the relationship is more complex when considering globalization's contribution to income inequality and inclusive growth.

This chapter explores the contribution of regional and extraregional linkages to the globalization process, and how these could impact key development outcomes. It first examines the relative contribution of regional integration, alongside that of integration outside the region, to global integration. Thereafter, it compares the effects of regional and global integration on economic outcomes—that is, if there is any suggestion they produce different results. The methodology used for this assessment is elaborated in Annex 4.

4.1   Contributions of Regional and Extraregional Integration to Global Integration

The Global Integration Index can be decomposed into two main components. The GII framework allows the index to be divided into two main components. The first is the Regional Integration Index (RII) which, as discussed in Chapter 3, was constructed in parallel with the GII. The RII is used to gauge an economy's socioeconomic linkages with other economies in the same region. RII is interchangeably referred to in this chapter as the index of regional or intraregional integration. The second component captures the gap between regional and global integration or an economy's socioeconomic linkages with economies outside its region. This is referred to as the extraregional integration index (EII). Together, the regional and extraregional integration indexes measure the level of global integration. The relative contributions of each can be important for policymakers, in particular when economies seek to balance their global economic linkages with geopolitical factors, strategic autonomy, and other considerations. It also provides additional information on vulnerabilities deriving from regional and global channels.

Regional, extraregional, and global integration linkages have increased since 2006. For the whole sample of 173 economies, regional linkages are not as strong as extraregional linkages, indicating that extraregional integration tends to have a greater pull (Figure 4.1). However, the relative contribution from each component for the full sample is similar and stable over the years (Figure 4.2). As stressed in previous chapters, notable declines in integration are associated with episodes of global economic turbulence such as the global financial crisis (2008–2009), the euro area debt crisis (2012–2013), and the COVID-19 pandemic (2019–2020). Regional and extraregional integration was also on the decline from 2015 to 2017, which could have reflected several events, including Brexit, monetary tightening by the Fed, the PRC's devaluation of the renminbi, and wild swings in oil prices.

Figure 4.1: Regional, Extraregional, and Global Integration Indexes—All Economies

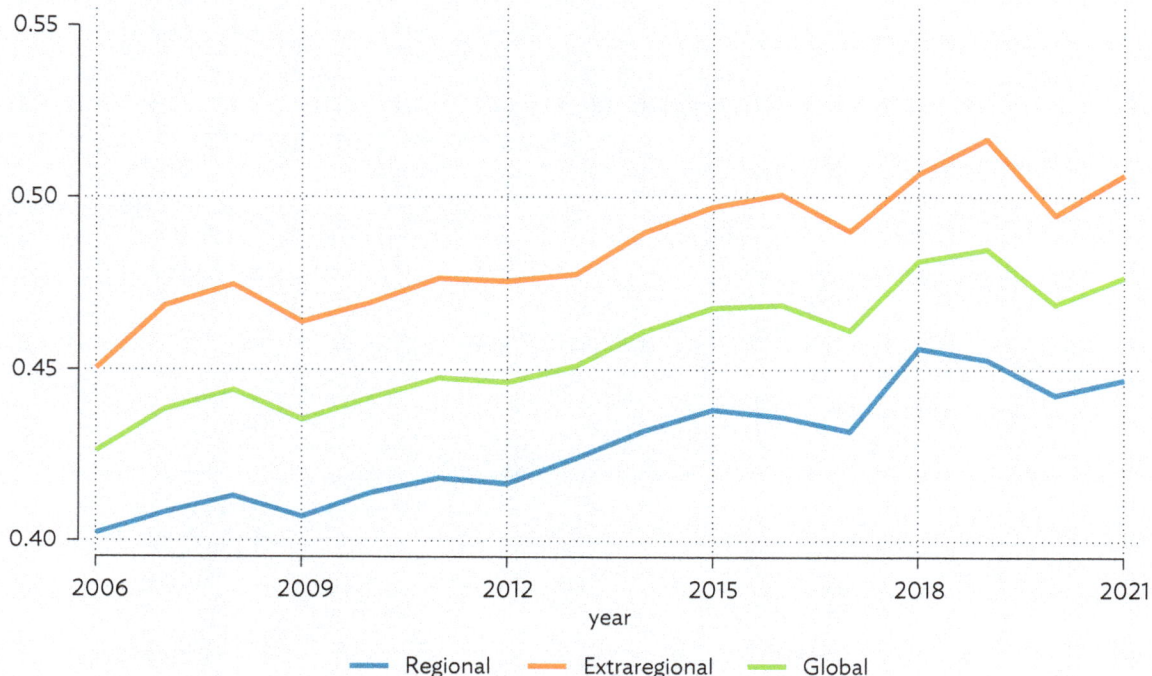

Note: Higher values denote greater integration. Data points are the average of all economies in the sample.

Source: ADB calculations using data from ADB. Asia-Pacific Regional Cooperation and Integration Index Database. https://aric.adb.org/database/arcii (accessed November 2023).

Regional and extraregional integration are similar in high-income economies while lower-income economies are more integrated extraregionally. On average, the gap between regional and extraregional integration in high-income economies is narrower than in low- and middle-income economies (Figure 4.3). Still, high-income economies are better integrated regionally compared to other income groups, also reflecting the important presence of the EU economies in this group. Low-income economies, in comparison, tend to be more integrated extraregionally. Although regional and extraregional integration make similar contributions to global integration, variations are observed across income groups. Global integration tends to be equally driven by regional and extraregional integration in high-income economies, whereas extraregional linkages are more important in other income groups. Also, on average for low-income economies, deeper extraregional linkages have been accompanied by stronger regional linkages.

Figure 4.2: Relative Contributions of Regional and Extraregional Linkages to Global Integration—All Economies

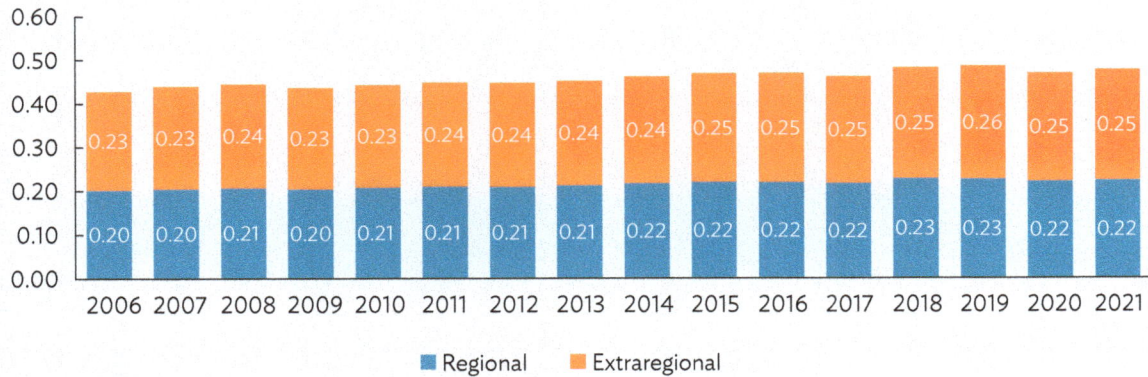

Note: Relative contribution is computed by multiplying the weight of the regional (extraregional) index by 0.5. Higher values denote greater contribution to global integration. Data points are the average of all economies in the sample.

Source: ADB calculations using data from ADB. Asia-Pacific Regional Cooperation and Integration Index Database. https://aric.adb.org/database/arcii (accessed November 2023).

Trends in regional and extraregional integration in Asia differ with other regions. The breakdown by region highlights some differences in the trajectory and contribution of regional and extraregional linkages. In Asia, integration with and outside the region has increased over time, with extraregional linkages slightly above regional linkages (Figure 4.4). In contrast, the EU and North America are more integrated regionally than with the outside. To some extent, estimates for the EU highlight the success of its regional integration process. In contrast, economies in Latin America and Africa are more integrated with partners outside their region than with their neighbors. For Latin America, structural factors such as high trade costs resulting from weak transportation and logistics infrastructure, insufficient trade facilitation, and regulatory constraints have been critical barriers to regional integration (Gonzales 2017; Acosta and de S. Paulo 2022). In Africa, intraregional integration has been hampered by insufficient infrastructure, political instability, non-convertibility of currencies, as well as binding ethnic, cultural, and linguistic diversity (Longo and Sekkat 2001; Foroutan and Pritchett 1993).

Overall, contributions of regional and extraregional integration to global integration are more balanced in Asia and the Pacific and North America. In the EU, deep regional ties contribute more to global integration than linkages outside the region. In Latin America and Africa, the level of global integration is strongly driven by linkages with economies outside the region. These trends highlight in particular the important role of regional linkages in the global integration of industrialized economies.

Figure 4.3: Regional, Extraregional, and Global Integration Indexes, by Income Group

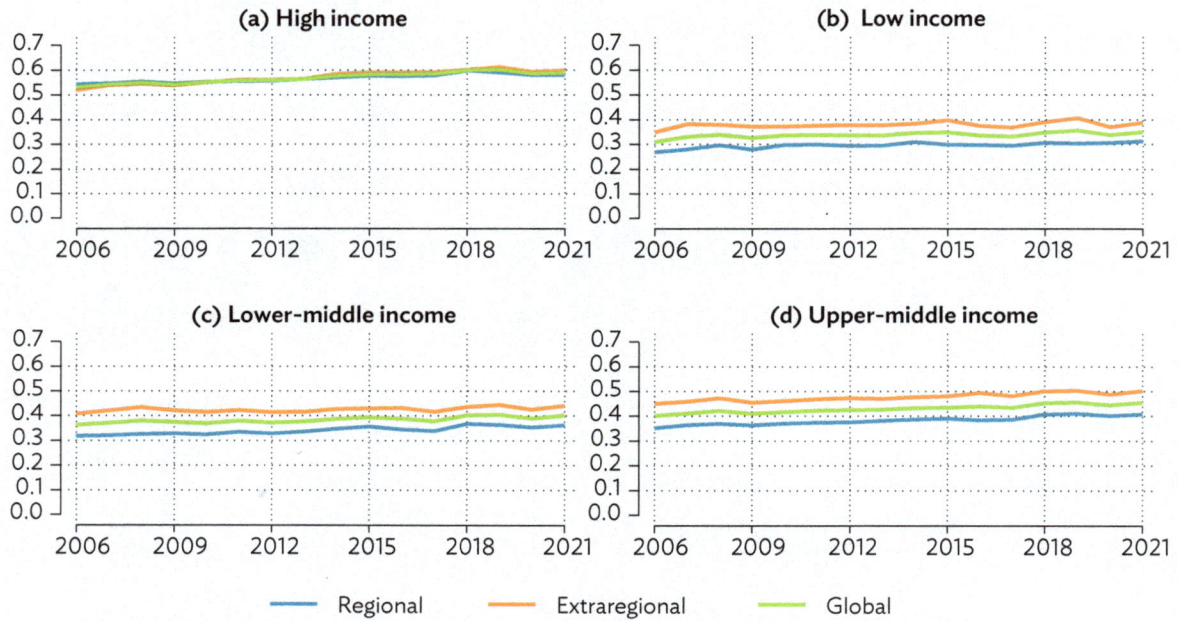

(a) High income

(b) Low income

(c) Lower-middle income

(d) Upper-middle income

Regional — Extraregional — Global

Sources: ADB calculations using data from ADB. Asia-Pacific Regional Cooperation and Integration Index Database. https://aric.adb. org/database/arcii; World Bank. World Development Indicators. https://databank.worldbank.org/source/world-developmentindicators (all accessed November 2023).

Figure 4.4: Regional, Extraregional, and Global Integration Indexes, by Region

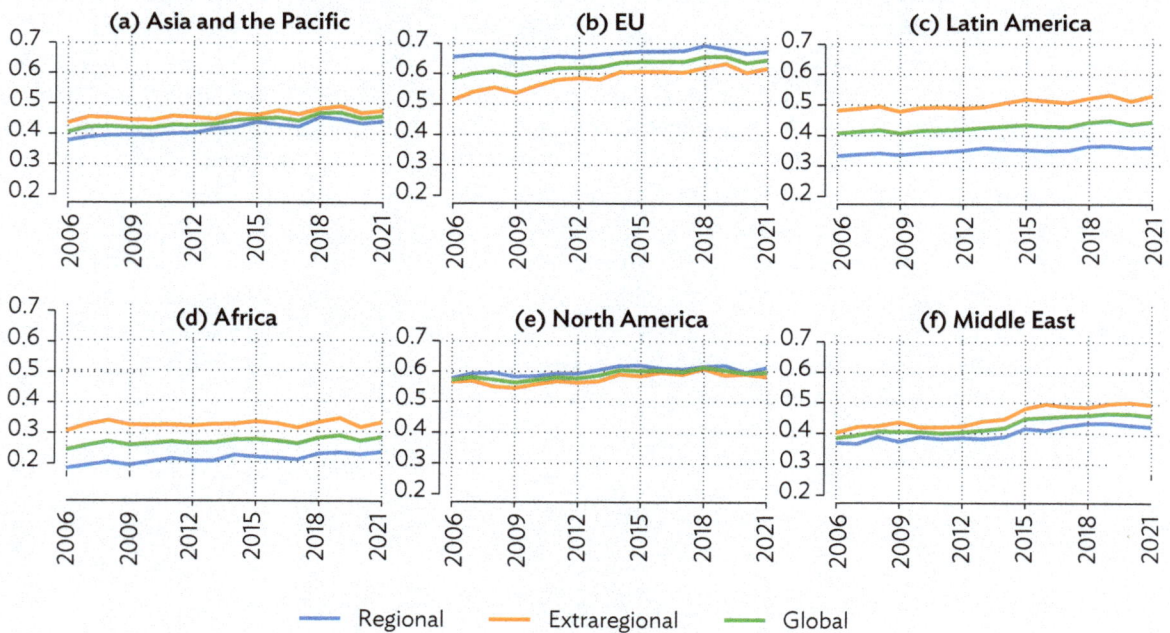

(a) Asia and the Pacific

(b) EU

(c) Latin America

(d) Africa

(e) North America

(f) Middle East

Regional — Extraregional — Global

EU = European Union.

Source: ADB calculations using data from ADB. Asia-Pacific Regional Cooperation and Integration Index Database. https://aric.adb. org/database/arcii (accessed November 2023).

4.2 Development Outcomes of Global and Regional Integration

The effects of globalization on development outcomes are complex and multifaceted, with multiple simultaneous channels needing to be considered. On one hand, globalization can increase economic growth by generating employment opportunities and improving living standards. On the other, globalization can exacerbate inequalities, undermine social welfare, and speed up climate change. With these effects in mind, regional integration has gained relevance, with its potential to serve as a cushion to the vulnerabilities presented by global integration. For one, regional integration may allow economies to reap the benefits of international trade without being exposed to risks from extraregional linkages. It can also help small-island economies overcome the difficulties from natural disadvantages and scale (Ding and Otker 2020).

Understanding the linkages between integration and development outcomes is critical for policymakers who aim to balance the pace of global and regional integration to achieve inclusive and sustainable growth. This section provides a brief overview of such linkages, particularly how they relate to economic growth, income inequality, and inclusive growth.

Economic Growth

Economic growth rates have fluctuated considerably across regions since 2006. Declines were particularly sharp in 2008–2009 and 2019–2020 due to the global financial crisis and the COVID-19 pandemic, and presented a big challenge to meeting the development targets, particularly poverty reduction targets (Figure 4.5). Research suggests that globalization could both promote or inhibit sustainable economic growth. On the one hand, globalization can promote growth through the expansion of foreign trade, together with gains in productivity, efficiency, and competition (Kılıçarslan and Dumrul 2018). At the same time, unmanaged global integration increases the transmission of external shocks and may only benefit certain groups.

Global (regional) integration and per capita GDP growth are positively associated. As Figure 4.6 shows, economies with a faster GII between 2006 and 2021 also reported faster growth in per capita income. This supports the notion that processes underlying global integration and development tend to coincide (Lang and Tavares 2018). The relationship between regional integration and per capita GDP growth is similar. Generally, Asian economies have high rates of growth in per capita income, with varying changes in global and regional integration. In comparison, most EU economies experienced slower per capita income growth and changes in integration in recent years, although they were already highly integrated.

The effects of global and regional integration on economic development may depend on relative factor endowments. For instance, Capello and Fratesi (2009) as mentioned in Polasek and Sellner (2013), showed in their simulation analysis that the impacts of globalization on regional growth and convergence depend on the region's ability to absorb external shocks and translate them into economic growth. Meanwhile, Gammadigbe (2021) notes that regional integration can bring benefits to more diverse and established economies serving as regional trading hubs, compared to those primarily based on agriculture or natural resources. As such, positive spillovers of global and regional integration may be muted where resources are lacking (e.g., infrastructure in the telecommunications sector).

Overall, findings suggest that global and regional integration can stimulate economic growth but economies may experience varying levels of growth. Economic gains from integration differ due to several possible factors, including an economy's depth of global and regional integration and its domestic policies for economic resilience and development.

Figure 4.5: GDP Growth Rates, by Region (%)

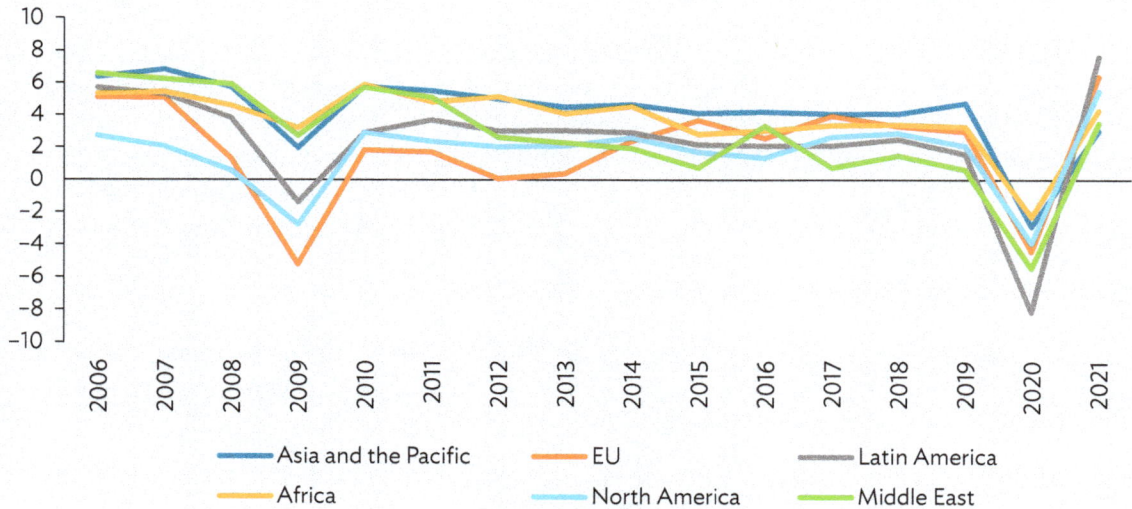

EU = European Union, GDP = gross domestic product.

Source: ADB calculations using data from World Bank. World Development Indicators. https://databank.worldbank.org/source/world-developmentindicators (accessed November 2023).

Figure 4.6: Correlation between Global (Regional) Integration and Economic Growth

(a) Global Integration Index

(b) Regional Integration Index

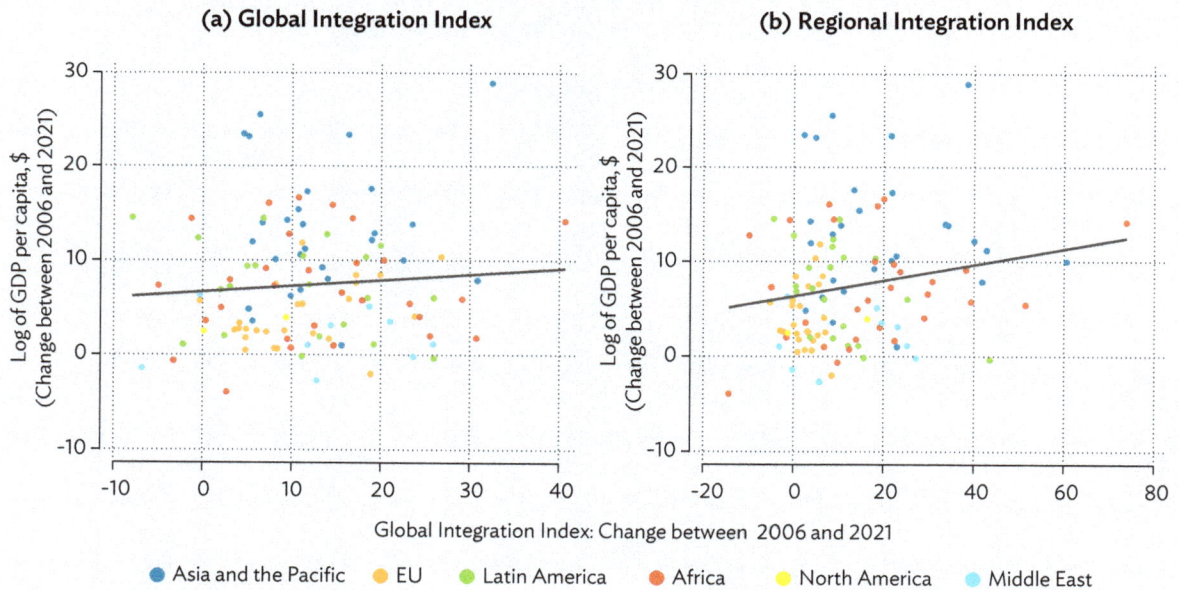

EU = European Union, GDP = gross domestic product.

Sources: ADB calculations using data from ADB. Asia-Pacific Regional Cooperation and Integration Index Database. https://aric.adb.org/database/arcii; World Bank. World Development Indicators. https://databank.worldbank.org/source/world-developmentindicators (all accessed November 2023).

Box 4.1: Economic Integration and Growth: Global and Regional Linkages

Empirical analyses on the relationship (and impacts) of global integration on economic growth have been widespread in the economic literature. The analysis in this section builds on this work, proposing an econometric specification to measure the linkages between economic growth and the global/regional integration indexes defined in Chapters 2 and 3. A group of structural factors from the literature were defined and considered in the specification. In most cases, the association between economic growth and these factors is as expected. Higher levels of lagged GDP per capita are associated with lower growth rates as a reflection of conditional convergence. Higher government consumption and fertility rates lead to lower growth rates. Growth rates are higher when there are more years of schooling and larger investments. An increase in the government effectiveness index leads to higher economic growth, and the same is true for the political stability index.

Empirical analysis suggests that GDP growth and global integration are positively associated. An increase of 1 percentage point in the Global Integration Index (GII) is associated with a 0.23 percentage point increase in GDP per capita (Figure 4.1.1, panel a). This is consistent with recent meta-analysis synthesizing the magnitude of the effect and suggesting a small-to-moderate positive impact of economic globalization on economic growth (Heimberger 2021). The results are also consistent when looking closely at income groups, although results for lower-middle and lower income groups are not statistically significant.[a]

At a regional level,[b] the positive effects of global integration on economic growth mainly apply to three regions: Asia and the Pacific, the EU, and Latin America (Figure 4.1.1, panel b). Results on linkages between regional integration and economic growth are also favorable for all regions except Africa (Figure 4.1.1, panel c). This supports the potential impact of regional integration through multiple channels, including economies of scale, market access, technology, and knowledge spillovers.

Figure 4.1.1: Global (Regional) Integration and Economic Growth

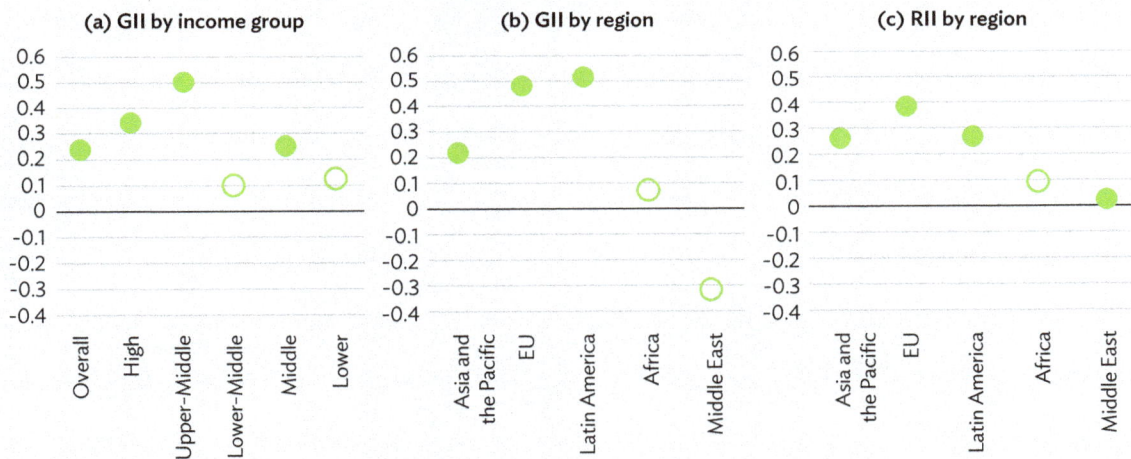

EU = European Union, GII = Global Integration Index, GDP = gross domestic product, RII = Regional Integration Index.

Notes: Dots describe regression coefficients assessing the association of the Global Integration Index and Regional Integration Index with economic growth, as represented by GDP growth. Hollow dots denote coefficients not significant at the 10% level.

Source: Huh et al. (forthcoming).

[a] Regression analysis was not performed for the low-income group because of the lack of usable data points. The low-income group had a small number of 22 economies, most with many missing values. To include low-income economies, auxilliary income groups were created: middle- and lower-income groups, where the former comprises upper- and lower-middle income economies, and the latter lower-middle and low-income economies.

[b] North America was excluded from the empirical analysis due to lack of data points since there are only two economies (i.e., the United States and Canada) within the region.

Source: Asian Development Bank.

Income Inequality

Recent trends show that income inequality persists across the globe. Based on the global Gini coefficient, global inequality reached two peaks, first around 1910 and then in 1980–2000 (Figure 4.7, panel a). While global inequality levels cascaded after 2008, it remains high in absolute terms, with 2020 levels comparable to the 1900s (Chancel and Piketty 2021). A breakdown of global inequality trends into components—within and between economies—provides a more compelling picture. Recent analysis suggests that levels of within-economy inequality have exceeded between-economy inequality in the early 2000s (Chancel et al. 2022). This suggests that income distribution within economies has become more important in determining global inequality, and that redistributive policies at the national level are crucial in reducing it. Latin America and Africa are the most unequal economies by income (Figure 4.7, panel b).

Figure 4.7: Trends in Inequality

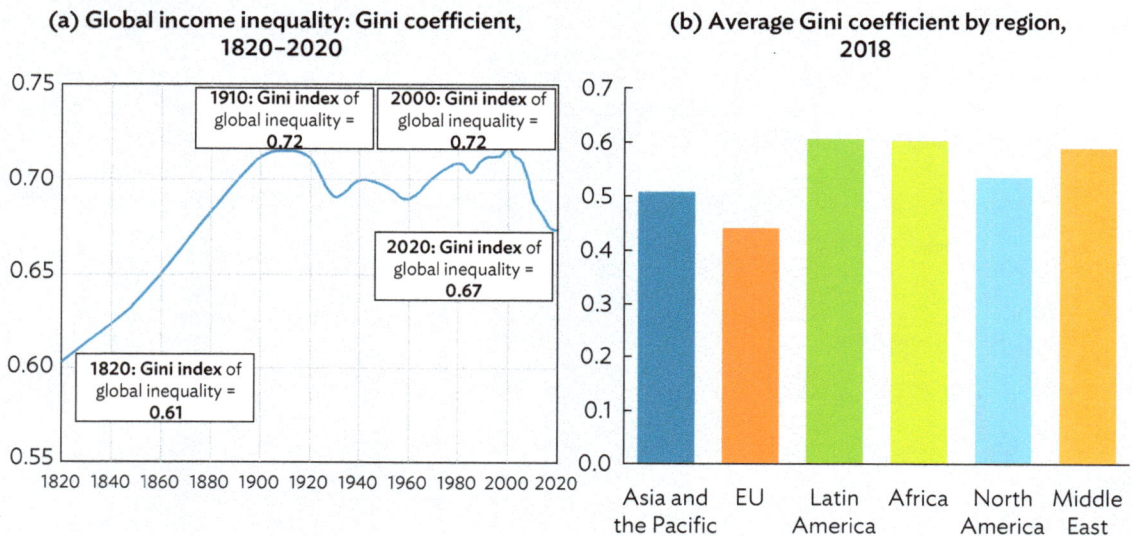

(a) Global income inequality: Gini coefficient, 1820–2020

1910: Gini index of global inequality = 0.72
2000: Gini index of global inequality = 0.72
2020: Gini index of global inequality = 0.67
1820: Gini index of global inequality = 0.61

(b) Average Gini coefficient by region, 2018

Asia and the Pacific, EU, Latin America, Africa, North America, Middle East

Note: Global income inequality measures inequality across the world population, regardless of nationality. The Gini coefficient ranges from 0 (perfect equality) to 1 (an individual captures all resources in an economy). Therefore, a higher Gini indicates higher inequality.

Source: Chancel, L. et al. 2022. *World Inequality Report 2022.* World Inequality Lab.

EU = European Union.

Note: The bars in panel (b) pertain to the average Gini coefficient (within-economies) across the regions.

Source: World Inequality database. https://wid.world/data/ (accessed July 2021).

Persistent income inequalities have cast doubt over the benefits of rapid global and regional integration. The relationship between global integration and income inequality, as expressed by the Gini Index, is not conclusive in itself (Figure 4.8, panel a). This is also true for regional integration and inequality (Figure 4.8, panel b). The weak correlation may somehow be explained by the diversity of outcomes of global and regional integration. For example, some advanced economies (e.g., France) have not experienced increasing inequality, while developing economies have experienced fluctuating trends in inequality (Schoder 2018).

The varying effects of global and regional integration on income inequality suggest that income levels matter. High-income economies can respond to the adverse effects of globalization, particularly among vulnerable workers. Rodrik (1998) and Bordo, Eichengreen, and Irwin (1999) noted that large welfare states increase transfers and subsidies to ensure that potential losers acquiesce to globalization. The same sense that global integration is not significant does not seem to apply to developing economies since it appears to have considerable adverse effects on income inequality. Kanbur (2000) and Attanasio, Goldberg, and Pavcnik (2004) concluded that increased openness from globalization coincides with increases in income inequality in developing economies.

As suggested, the association between global (regional) integration and income inequality remains debatable. There is no clear evidence that globalization affects income inequality, given that several other underlying factors may alleviate or exacerbate inequality. Regardless of their depth of integration, economies may have the domestic means to tackle inequality issues, such as through labor regulations and redistributive tax and transfer systems. A more important question therefore concerns how the effects of globalization and regionalization are distributed across different income groups.

Figure 4.8: Integration and Trends in Income Inequality

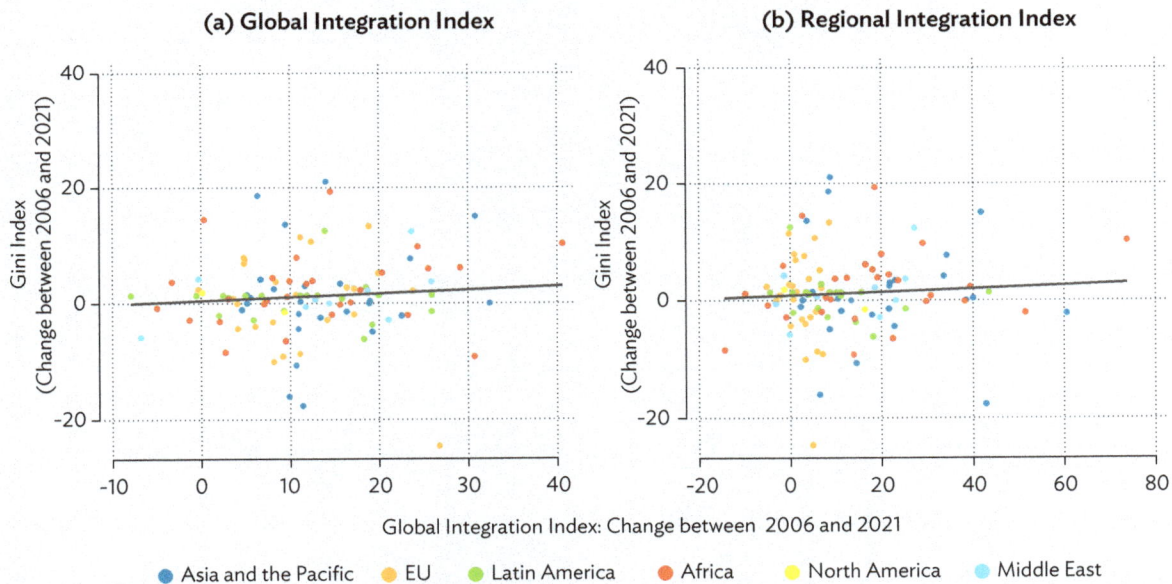

(a) Global Integration Index

(b) Regional Integration Index

Global Integration Index: Change between 2006 and 2021

● Asia and the Pacific ● EU ● Latin America ● Africa ● North America ● Middle East

EU = European Union.

Sources: ADB calculations from ADB. Asia-Pacific Regional Cooperation and Integration Index Database. https://aric.adb.org/database/arcii; World Inequality Lab. World Inequality database. https://wid.world/data/ (accessed November 2023).

Box 4.2: Economic Integration and Income Inequality: Global and Regional Linkages

Income inequality is influenced by different variables. In most regions, schooling, accountability, GDP per capita, government transfer and subsidies, and domestic credit to the private sector reduce income inequality while unemployment worsens it. There are some exceptions in the direction of the effects, but most are not statistically significant.

Findings from our own empirical analysis suggest that global integration significantly worsens income inequality in some groups. For instance, an increase in GII of one point is associated with higher income inequality (as measured by the Gini Index from the World Inequality Database)[a] among high income 0.07 percentage points (Figure 4.2.1, panel a). The opposite is true for lower-income groups. By region, global integration yields similar implications for almost all regions, although results were only significant for Africa (Figure 4.2.1, panel b). As such, global integration tends to lower income inequality, except for Asia and the Pacific. On the other hand, regional integration tends to have more heterogenous effects although the results were significant only for the Middle East region (Figure 4.2.1, panel c).

Figure 4.2.1: The Relationship between Global (Regional) Integration and Income Inequality

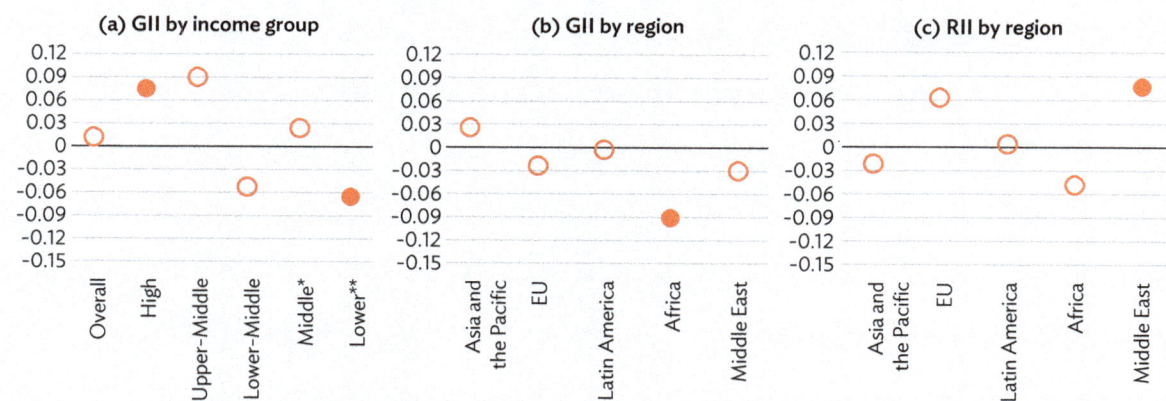

*Upper and lower-middle income, **Lower-middle and low income, EU = European Union, GII = Global Integration Index, RII = Regional Integration Index.

Notes: Dots describe regression coefficients assessing the association of Global Integration Index with income inequality (using the Gini Index developed by the World Inequality Database). Hollow dots denote coefficients not significant at 10% level.

Source: Huh et al. (forthcoming).

[a] Another measure of the Gini index is available at the World Development Indicators (WDI) of the World Bank. However, the WDI has poor economy coverage: for example, merely 59 economies from our sample. The WDI has wider data coverage and includes 151 economies from our sample.

Source: Asian Development Bank.

Inclusive Growth

While developing economies experienced high growth rates in recent years, the benefits tend to be unequally distributed. Inclusive growth is not solely determined by income inequality. It also encompasses other aspects such as equality in employment opportunities, health outcomes, and education outcomes. Consistent with the earlier finding on income inequality, the EU on average is most inclusive (Figure 4.9). While Asia and the Pacific follows, inclusive growth estimates for the region are wider in distribution.

Figure 4.9: Inclusive Growth Index, 2020

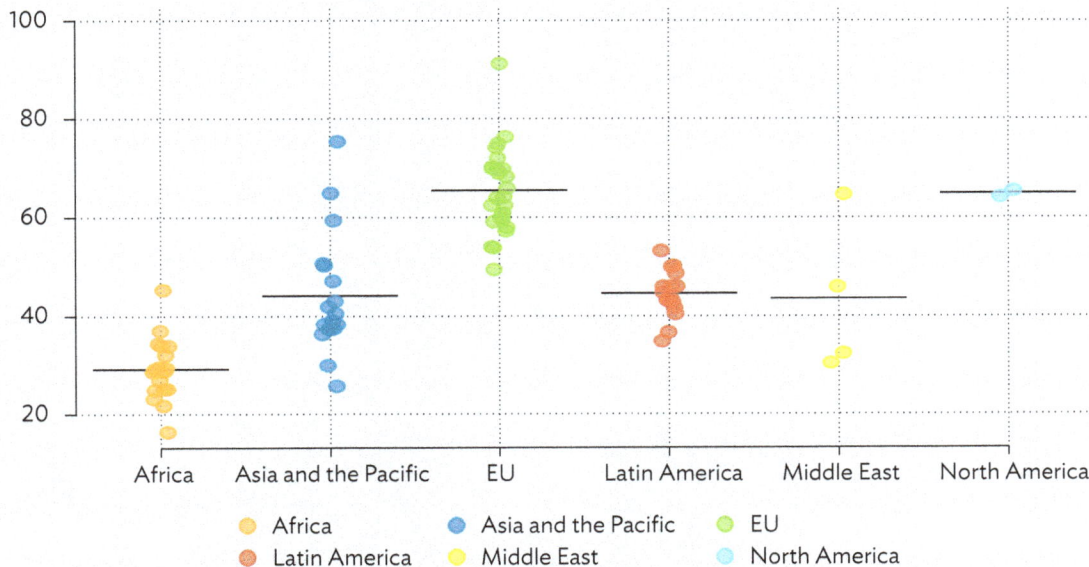

EU = European Union.

Note: The gray line represents the average for each region. The dots represent economy estimates from UNCTAD's Inclusive Growth Index (2022). The index has four pillars: economy, living conditions, equality, and environment.

Source: ADB estimates using data from UNCTAD. 2022. SDG Pulse. https://sdgpulse.unctad.org/inclusive-growth/ (accessed November 2022).

It is useful to examine whether global and/or regional integration deepens inclusive growth, as this indicator considers the linkages between economic growth and income inequality. High inequality in income can dampen economic growth through various mechanisms (Aoyagi and Ganelli 2015; Anand, Mishra, and Peiris 2013). The Organisation for Economic Co-operation and Development concludes that the long-term trend increase in income inequality has curbed economic growth significantly in its members (OECD 2014). One implication is that economic growth needs to effectively reduce income inequality to be sustainable.

The relationship between global (regional) integration and inclusive growth is far from straightforward. In an ideal scenario, economic growth induced by global and regional integration could reduce poverty and result in a more equitable distribution of income or economic opportunities. However, that is not always so, as greater integration may also induce wider disparities. For example, trade integration may lead to widening social inequalities if no proper measures are in place to safeguard workers from the shocks of increased international competition (ILO 1999). Descriptive evidence shows that the relationship between global integration and inclusive growth is positive, while slightly negative for regional integration, although the association appears to be weak (Figure 4.10).[7]

---

[7] In the literature, a simple form of inclusive growth is growth adjusted for income inequality, representing equitable income growth. In this exercise, a simple form of inclusive growth is used following Atkinson (1970) where economic growth adjusted for income inequality. We use "inclusive growth" and "equitable income growth" interchangeably, although inclusive growth has stood for a wide spectrum of equitable growth, interspersed with equity issues like gender equity, income equity, education equality, race equality, and so on. A more holistic measure of inclusive growth may be constructed, for example, based on composite indexes to capture various aspects of inclusiveness (e.g., McKinley 2010).

Figure 4.10: Correlation between Global (Regional) Integration and Inclusive Growth

(a) Global Integration Index	(b) Regional Integration Index

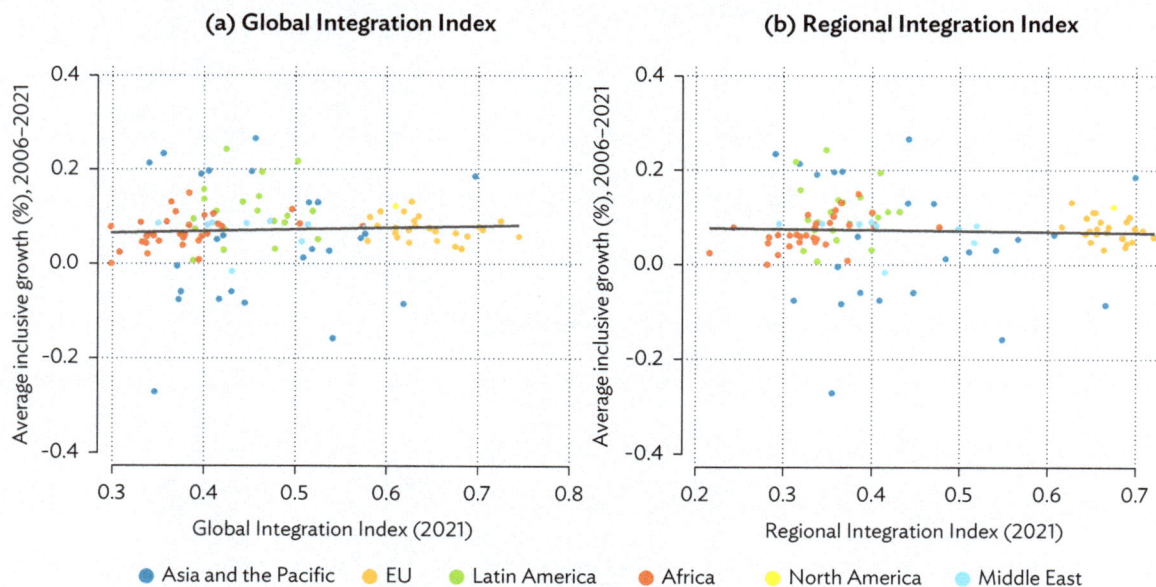

EU = European Union.

Note: Inclusive growth rates are calculated based on the methodology described in Box 4.3.

Sources: ADB calculations from ADB. Asia-Pacific Regional Cooperation and Integration Index Database. https://aric.adb.org/database/arcii (accessed November 2023); World Inequality Lab. World Inequality database. https://wid.world/data/ (accessed November 2023).

Box 4.3: Computation of the Inclusive Growth Indicator

The measure of inclusive growth is constructed using Atkinson's (1970) inequality index for income distribution. The World Inequality Database provides income distribution for 151 economies in our sample based on pretax per-capita real national income for adults. An Atkinson inequality index is computed using percentiles of this income distribution, which measures the share of total income that a society must forego to have equally distributed incomes. It is bounded between zero and one, and a higher value implies more inequality in the income distribution. The aversion parameter (ε) in the formula is set to one, as also adopted by the Inequality-adjusted Human Development Index (IHDP) of the United Nations Development Programme (2020). By increasing ε, the value of the Atkinson inequality index also rises, implying that society needs to give up increasing shares of total income in order to achieve equality in incomes.

The Atkinson inequality index then becomes $AK = 1 - (g/a) = 1 - (\sqrt[n]{y_1 \cdot y_2 \cdots y_n}/\overline{y})$, where g is the geometric average and a is the arithmetic averages of the income distribution, and y_i is the ith percentile income. The results show that Chile has the most unequal distribution of income. Its AK has a value in the range of 0.913 to 0.976 from 2006 to 2021, with an average of 0.928. The Czech Republic exhibits the least unequal income distribution, in which the AK value resides in the range of 0.290 to 0.320, with an average of 0.303. Inclusive income is obtained by multiplying the income by (1-AK), and its growth rate is used as a measure of inclusive growth.

Alternatively, Anand, Mishra, and Peiris (2013) proposes an income equality index based on a utilitarian social welfare function for measuring inclusive growth. This index of income equality lies between zero and one, with a higher value being more equal in the income distribution. In our sample, the cross correlation between the Atkinson inequality index and the equality index by Anand, Mishra, and Peiris (2013) is −0.973, suggesting that the two measures are virtually identical in practice.

Source: Asian Development Bank.

Box 4.4: Economic Integration and Inclusive Growth: Global and Regional Linkages

Building on the econometric approach for growth and income inequality, ADB's estimation results show that inclusive growth is negatively associated with lagged GDP per capita, government consumption, and unemployment rate. It is positively associated with domestic investment, government expenditure on education, and index of labor market regulation. In most cases, other factors influence economic growth in line with expectations. The lagged GDP per capita shows a negative sign to ensure conditional convergence in all regions. Higher economic growth is associated with higher domestic investment, political stability, and government effectiveness—and a low level of government consumption, irrespective of regional or global integration. Schooling and fertility rate produce somewhat mixed results, as the sign and statistical significance of the individual coefficients vary depending on the equation.

The results of our empirical exercise suggest that while globalization tends to be positively correlated with income inequality for some groups, it is also associated with increased inclusiveness, consistent with the findings of Gozgor and Ranjan (2017). Moreover, individual and cross-economy analysis by Dollar and Kraay (2004) suggests that in economies with open trade regimes, income growth leads to poverty reduction. However, while global integration is positively associated with inclusive growth across almost all income groups, the increase is the largest and is statistically significant only in the high-income group (Figure 4.4.1, panel a).

The analysis by region shows that the improvement in the inclusiveness of growth owing to global integration is significant only in the EU and Africa (Figure 4.4.1, panel b). Redistribution policies, redistributive taxes, as well as broad social protection coverage may enable many European economies to cushion the negative effects of globalization on income disparities (Blanchet, Chancel, and Gethin 2019; European Economic and Social Committee 2018; Lang and Tavares 2018b). The European Globalisation Adjustment Fund for Displaced Workers (EGF) is also a promising initiative to promote inclusivity in the labor market, by helping displaced and disadvantaged workers find employment (European Commission n.d.). Finally, regional integration tends to be positively related to inclusive growth, particularly in the EU and Africa where the estimates were found to be significant (Figure 4.4.1, panel c).

Figure 4.4.1: The Relationship between Global (Regional) Integration and Inclusive Growth

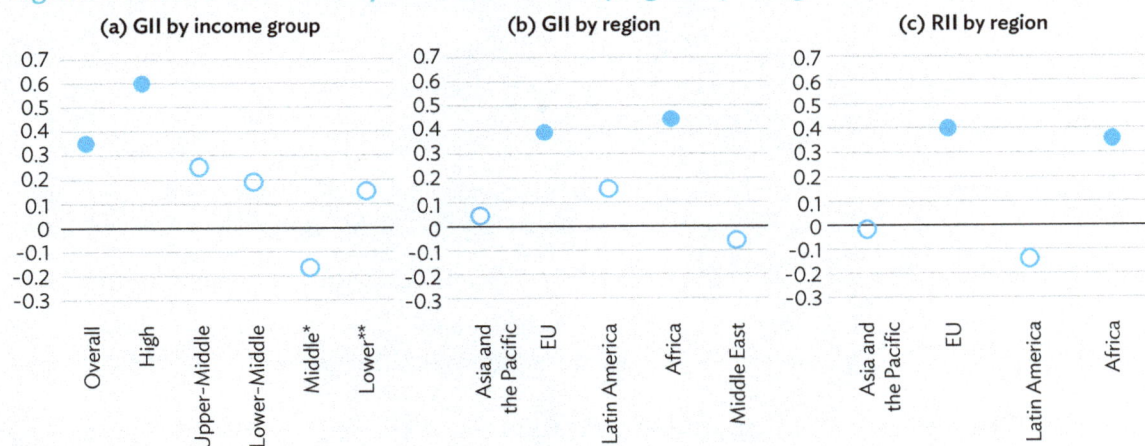

*Upper and lower-middle income, **Lower-middle and low income, EU = European Union, GII = Global Integration Index, RII = Regional Integration Index.

Notes: Dots describe regression coefficients assessing the association of Global Integration Index with inclusive growth (defined by growth adjusted for income inequality). Hollow dots denote coefficients not significant at the 10% level.

Source: Huh et al. (forthcoming).

References

Acosta, P. and F. de S. Paulo. 2022. Trade, Regional Integration and Collaboration: An Agenda for Brazil and Latin America. World Bank Opinion. 16 June. https://www.worldbank.org/en/news/opinion/2022/06/16/comercio-integracao-regional-e-colaboracao-uma-agenda-para-o-brasil-e-a-america-latina (accessed 23 November 2022).

Anand, R., S. Mishra, and S. J. Peiris. 2013. Inclusive Growth: Measurement and Determinants. *IMF Working Paper.* 13 (135). Washington, DC: International Monetary Fund. https://www.imf.org/external/pubs/ft/wp/2013/wp13135.pdf.

Antràs, P. 2020. De-globalisation? Global Value Chains in the Post-COVID-19 Age. *NBER Working Paper Series.* 28115. Cambridge, MA: National Bureau of Economic Research. http://www.nber.org/papers/w28115.

Aoyagi, C. and G. Ganelli. 2015. Asia's Quest for Inclusive Growth Revisited. *IMF Working Paper.* 15 (42). Washington, DC: International Monetary Fund. https://www.imf.org/external/pubs/ft/wp/2015/wp1542.pdf.

Asian Development Bank (ADB). 2018. *Strategy 2030: Achieving a Prosperous, Inclusive, Resilient, and Sustainable Asia and the Pacific.* Manila. doi:http://dx.doi.org/10.22617/TCS189401-2.

Atkinson, A. B. 1970. On the Measurement of Inequality. *Journal of Economic Theory.* 2 (3). pp. 244–63. doi: https://doi.org/10.1016/0022-0531(70)90039-6.

Attanasio, O., P. K. Goldberg, and N. Pavcnik. 2004. Trade Reforms and Wage Inequality in Colombia. *Journal of Development Economics.* 74 (2). pp. 331–366.

Barro, R. 1997. *Determinants of Economic Growth: A Cross-Country Empirical Study.* Cambridge: MIT Press.

Blanchet, T., L. Chancel, and A. Gethin. 2019. *Forty Years of Inequality in Europe: Evidence from Distribitional National Accounts.* 22 April. https://cepr.org/voxeu/columns/fortyyears-inequality-europe-evidence-distributional-national-accounts (accessed 9 November 2022).

Bordo, M. D., B. Eichengreen, and D. A. Irwin. 1999. Is Globalization Today Really Different than Globalization a Hunderd Years Ago? *NBER Working Papers.* 7195. Cambridge, MA: National Bureau of Economic Research. https://ideas.repec.org/p/nbr/nberwo/7195.html.

Capello, R. and U. Fratesi. 2009. Globalization and a Dual Europe: Future Alternative Growth Trajectories. *The Annals of Regional Science.* 45. pp. 633–65. doi:https://doi.org/10.1007/s00168-009-0295-6.

Chancel, L. and T. Piketty. 2021. Global Income Inequality, 1820–2020: The Persistence and Mutation of Extreme Inequality. *Journal of the European Economic Association.* 19 (6). pp. 3025–62. doi:https://doi.org/10.1093/jeea/jvab047.

Chancel, L., T. Piketty, E. Saez, and G. Zucman. 2022. *World Inequality Report 2022. World Inequality Database.* https://wir2022.wid.world/www-site/uploads/2023/03/D_FINAL_WIL_RIM_RAPPORT_2303.pdf.

Ding, D. and I. Otker. 2020. Strengthening Caribbean Regional Integration. *International Monetary Fund.* 4 February. https://www.imf.org/en/News/Articles/2020/02/04/NA020420-Strengthening-Caribbean-Regional-Integration (accessed 13 December 2022).

Dollar, D. and A. Kraay. 2004. Trade, Growth, and Poverty. *The Economic Journal.* 114 (493). pp. 22–49.

European Commission. n.d. *European Globalisation Adjustment Fund for Displaced Workers (EGF).* https://ec.europa.eu/social/main.jsp?catId=326&langId=en (accessed 9 November 2022).

European Economic and Social Committee. 2018. *The European Social Model: Can We Still Afford It in This Globalised World?* Brussels. doi:doi:10.2864/35970.

Foroutan, F. S. and L. H. Pritchett. 1993. Intra-sub-Saharan African Trade: Is It Too Little? *Policy Research Working Paper.* 1225. Washington, DC: World Bank. https://documents.worldbank.org/en/publication/documents-reports/documentdetail/893661468742854445/intra-sub-saharan-african-trade-is-it-too-little.

Gammadigbe, V. 2021. Is Regional Trade Integration a Growth and Convergence Engine in Africa? *IMF Working Papers.* 21 (19). Washington, DC: International Monetary Fund. https://www.imf.org/en/Publications/WP/Issues/2021/01/29/Is-Regional-Trade-Integration-a-Growth-and-Convergence-Engine-in-Africa-50040.

García-Herrero, A. 2020. From Globalization to Deglobalization: Zooming into Trade. https://www.bruegel.org/sites/default/files/wp-content/uploads/2020/02/Globalization-desglobalization.pdf (accessed 13 December 2022).

Gonzales, A. 2017. 3 Challenges Latin American Economies Must Overcome to Boost Intraregional Trade. World Bank Blog. 28 March. https://blogs.worldbank.org/trade/3-challengeslatin-american-economies-must-overcome-boost-intraregional-trade (accessed 23 November 2022).

Gozgor, G. and P. Ranjan. 2017. Globalisation, Inequality and Redistribution: Theory and Evidence. *The World Economy.* 40 (12). pp. 2704–51. doi:https://doi.org/10.1111/twec.12518.

Heimberger, P. 2021. Does Economic Globalisation Promote Economic Growth? A Meta-analysis. *The World Economy.* 45 (6). pp. 1690–712 doi:https://doi.org/10.1111/twec.13235.

Huh, H-S., C-Y. Park, R. Avendano, and L. Tolin. Forthcoming. Global and Regional Integration and their Economic Implications: Evidence from a New Integration Index.

International Monetary Fund (IMF). 2018. *World Economic Outlook: Challenges to a Steady Growth.* Washington, DC. https://www.imf.org/en/Publications/WEO/Issues/2018/09/24/world-economic-outlook-october-2018.

International Labour Organization (ILO). 1999. Globalization Boosts Economic Growth but Risks Widening Social Inequality. *News.* 19 November. https://www.ilo.org/global/about-the-ilo/newsroom/news/WCMS_007960/lang--en/index.htm (accessed 13 December 2022).

Jain-Chandra, S., T. Kinda, K. Kochhar, S. Piao, and J. Schauer. 2016. Sharing the Growth Dividend: Analysis of Inequality in Asia. *IMF Working Paper*. 048. Washington, DC: International Monetary Fund. https://www. imf.org/en/Publications/WP/Issues/2016/12/31/Sharing-the-Growth-Dividend-Analysis-of-Inequality-in-Asia-43767.

Kanbur, R. 2000. Income Distribution and Development. In A. Atkinson and F. Bourguignon, eds. *Handbook of Income Distribution*. pp. 791–841. https://econpapers.repec.org/bookchap/eeeincchp/1-13.htm.

Kılıcarslan, Z. and Y. Dumrul. 2018. The Impact of Globalization on Economic Growth: Empirical Evidence from the Türkiye. *International Journal of Economics and Financial Issues*. 8 (5). pp. 115–23. https://www.econjournals.com/index.php/ijefi/article/view/6593.

Kim, H-M., P. Li, and Y. R. Lee. 2020. Observations of Deglobalization against Globalization and Impacts. *International Trade, Politics and Development*. 4 (2). Emerald Publishing Limited. https://www.emerald.com/insight/2586-3932.htm.

Lang, V. and M. M. Tavares. 2018a. *How Income Gains from Globalisation are Distributed*. Center for Economic and Policy Research. 27 April. https://cepr.org/voxeu/columns/howincome-gains-globalisation-are-distributed (accessed 9 November 2022).

————. 2018b. The Distribution of Gains from Globalization. *International Monetary Fund Working Paper*. No. 2018/054. Washington, DC: IMF. https://www.imf.org/en/Publications/WP/Issues/2018/03/13/The-Distribution-of-Gains-from-Globalization-45722.

Longo, R. and K. Sekkat. 2001. Obstacles to Expanding Intra-African Trade. *OECD Development Centre Working Papers*. Paris: OECD Publishing. 169. doi:https://doi.org/10.1787/042583120128.

Organisation for Economic Co-operation and Development (OECD). 2014. *Focus on Inequality and Growth*. Paris. https://www.oecd.org/social/Focus-Inequality-and-Growth-2014.pdf.

Polasek, W. and R. Sellner. 2013. Does Globalization Affect Regional Growth? Evidence for NUTS-2 Regions in EU-27. *DANUBE: Law and Economics Review*. (1). pp. 23–65. https://www-sre.wu.ac.at/ersa/ersaconfs/ersa11/e110830aFinal00819.pdf.

Rodrik, D. 1998. Why Do More Open Economies Have Bigger Governments? *Journal of Political Economy*. 106 (5). pp. 997–1032. doi:https://doi.org/10.1086/250038.

Schoder, D. 2018. *Is a Globalized World a Less Equal World?* American Economic Association. 15 June. https://www.aeaweb.org/research/globalization-income-inequality-trade-policy (accessed 13 December 2022).

United Nations Development Programme. 2020. Human Development Report 2020: Technical Note. New York.

Vamvakidis, A. 1998. Regional Integration and Economic Growth. *The World Bank Economic Review*. (2). pp. 251–270. https://www.jstor.org/stable/3990091 (accessed 10 November 2022).

World Bank. 2016. *Poverty and Shared Prosperity 2016: Taking on Inequality*. Washington DC: World Bank. https://openknowledge.worldbank.org/handle/10986/25078 (accessed 6 December 2022).

Annex 4.1: Methodology in Calculating the Impact of Global (Regional) Integration on Development Outcomes

Extensive literature on globalization has delved into its relationship with development outcomes, particularly economic growth and income inequality. However, studies often rely on proxy variables that only capture specific dimensions of globalization, potentially leading to incomplete assessments of its overall impact on economic growth and income inequality. This limitation may arise from the omission of crucial dimensions, introducing bias into the reported effects. Moreover, the interconnectedness of various globalization dimensions makes their individual inclusion in regression analysis problematic due to collinearity issues.

To overcome these shortcomings, Dreher et al. (2008) introduced a composite index that consolidates multiple facets of globalization into a unified measure. This approach proves especially valuable when studying income inequality, where institutional and economic factors come into play. Institutional factors emphasize the necessity of a comprehensive globalization measure rather than a single proxy when investigating its effects on income inequality (Dreher et al. 2008).

In line with this methodology, the analysis in section 4.2 explores the impact of globalization on economic growth and income inequality, utilizing the composite indexes presented in this report. An economy fixed effects model (panel regression) is employed to account for time-invariant unobservable heterogeneity potentially correlated with explanatory variables. The Globalization Integration Index (GII) and Regional Integration Index (RII) serve as explanatory variables in each regression, assessing their influence on economic growth, income inequality, and inclusive growth. Additionally, other control variables are integrated to account for potential confounding factors.

Endogeneity Issue of Economic Integration

All panel regressions used standard ordinary least squares within a single equation setup. However, a concern with this method is the potential endogeneity of global and regional integration. Despite including numerous control variables, unaccounted factors could affect both integration and economic growth, leading to biased estimates. For example, in the analysis in section 4.2, a likely source of endogeneity is reverse causality: economic growth driving global/regional integration. As economies grow, they tend to globalize or regionalize more. Economic growth attracts foreign and domestic investors, while governments implement policies like infrastructure development, institutional reforms, and tax incentives to foster global and regional engagement.

To account for possible endogeneity between economic growth and globalization, Lang and Tavares (2018) suggest an instrumental variable (IV) approach, in which the instrument at work is an inverse-distance weighted average of the lagged globalization scores. This approach was based on two underlying premises. First, globalization is transmitted across borders, particularly between geographically close economies, with a one-period transmission lag. Second, globalization in neighboring economies affects an economy's income levels and distribution only through globalization. Following Lang and Tavares (2018), the instrument of the GII for economy i in year t, $GII_{i,t}^{IV}$, can be defined as

$$GII_{i,t}^{IV} = \left[\sum_{j \neq i}\left(\frac{1}{distance_{ij}} \times GII_{j,t-1}\right)\right] \Bigg/ \left[\sum_{j \neq i}\left(\frac{1}{distance_{ij}}\right)\right]$$

where the geographic distance between two economies i and j $distance_{ij}$ ($distance_{ij}$) is the population-adjusted distance between the main agglomerations of the two economies produced by Mayer and Zignago (2011). For the RII, the corresponding instrument, $RII_{i,t}^{IV}$, is defined in the same manner, except that partner economy j is in the same region. Once the instrument is constructed, the two-stage least squares technique can be employed for estimation, where GII (RII) in the regression is substituted by fitted values of the first-stage regression of GII (RII) on its instrument GII^{IV} (RII^{IV}) and all other explanatory variables, including the set of economy fixed effects. Addressing this issue of endogeneity will be the focus of upcoming work (Huh et al. forthcoming), paving the way for a more comprehensive exploration of the implications of global and regional integration.

CHAPTER 5
Conclusion

Globalization is multifaceted and complex in nature, and its definition is constantly changing. Recent geopolitical tensions and supply chain disruptions point to a rethinking of globalization as a model. These recent trends warrant more detailed measurements of global economic integration that can deepen understanding of its costs and benefits. That is the value proposition for use of the composite index on Global Integration Index (GII) and a Regional Integration Index (RII) highlighted throughout this report. Since the RII and GII share a framework, users can compare global and regional integration on the same footing across a number of dimensions. The report also assesses the contribution of regional integration to global integration and proposes applications for exploring the relationship between integration and development outcomes.

The results suggest that both global and regional integration strengthened between 2006 to 2021. They also shared similar patterns and channels. Levels of global integration are strongly linked to economic development, with highest estimates in the higher income groups. Geographically, the index reveals different trajectories, with Asia and the Pacific being less globally integrated than the EU but more integrated than other emerging-economy regions.

The relationship between global economic integration and development outcomes such as economic growth and income inequality is complicated and requires careful consideration. The evidence does not offer conclusive proof that integration efforts diminish inequality or promote inclusive growth, since these outcomes may be attributed to other underlying factors, including domestic policies, that have more direct impact. This highlights the need for further research on the impacts of globalization and regional integration based on comprehensive, evidence-based metrics such as the ones proposed in this report.

This report stresses that globalization continues to deepen despite recent trends of geopolitical tensions, supply chain disruptions, and financial crises. Contrary to the narrative that a period of deglobalization has begun, international capital flows are neither reversing nor is there compelling evidence of economic fragmentation into rival blocs. Globalization continues to contribute to expanding markets, improving resource allocation efficiency and boosting productivity and investment opportunities. Governments and policymakers need to combine global and regional integration efforts with domestic policies for sustainable and inclusive economic growth. These policies should include solid labor regulatory frameworks and redistributive tax and transfer systems, with the goal of distributing the benefits of global and regional integration efficiently and inclusively.

Regional economic integration continues to strengthen as economies recognize its benefits. In Asia and the Pacific, economic leaders have committed to open, strengthen, and develop trade and investment. The region accounted for over one-third of global flows in goods trade in 2021 despite feeling the effects of the pandemic from the previous year. Economies in Asia and the Pacific have also spearheaded heavy investment in technology, innovation, and research and development, as evidenced by a large proportion of patents filed. This underscores the view that regional integration may be a stepping-stone to globalization, wherein economies can test their products in regional markets, enhance liberalization process, and increase their capacity to integrate to global markets. Findings likewise suggest that growing extraregional linkages have helped foster global integration for most income groups.

Last, this report recognizes that the globalization and regionalization processes are intertwined and often mutually dependent processes. The GII and RII together provide a useful tool for informed policy decisions pertinent to integration-oriented policies. For one, the indexes can serve as metrics allowing users to track the level of global and regional integration, while providing insights on whether policies targeting it have been effective. Also, this tool can be used in research to examine the potential benefits and costs of regionalization and globalization across multiple dimensions, including distributional or environmental outcomes. Better integration metrics can be a first step for these initiatives to be inclusive, sustainable, and beneficial for all stakeholders.